YELLOW-GREEN VASELINE!

A GUIDE TO THE MAGIC GLASS

REVISED EDITION

BY

JAY GLICKMAN

AND

TERRY FEDOSKY

"Valuable is the word for Vaseline as this particular glass has acquired a legion of admirers over the years."

— Dan D'Imperio
The ABC's of Victorian Antiques

DEDICATION

*This book is respectfully dedicated to the late William R. Fescina,
a gentle man with a love and respect for things of the past, for his
encouragement in helping the author feel that he was not alone in
his obsession with the antique arts.*

— Jay L. Glickman

ACKNOWLEDGMENTS

My thanks and gratitude to Anita F. Steiner, without whose loving help and guidance this book would not have been possible.

Thanks also to Dr. Brian Redmond for his invaluable technical assistance.

My gratitude also to Mr. Frank M. Fenton, retired Chairman of the Board of the Fenton Art Glass Co., as well as the late writer and glass historian William Heacock, both of whom helped greatly in this endeavor.

— Jay L. Glickman

Thanks to David Richardson, who gave me the opportunity to work on this book and also travelled to Kentucky to do the photography himself. My gratitude is also extended to Terry Nutter, who had her work cut out for her, trying to keep me on track. Special thanks to Tom O'Connor, who helped pull it all together.

This revision couldn't have been done without the help of Jerry and Carol Snook, Madolyn Courter, Jerry Chambers, Hal Hooper, Jackie Shirley, and Libby Yalom. Special thanks to Mr. Frank M. Fenton, who assisted me with corrections for pictured Fenton pieces, as well as corrections in the chapters.

Also, thanks to Jay Glickman, who started it all.

Last, but not least, thanks to my family for their encouragement and support — Roger and Carolyn Fedosky, Vicki Cope, Jeff Fedosky, Gary "Bugs" Fedosky, Patrick Young, Shannon Young and Dennis Cope, and Rhiannon Taylor. My appreciation also goes to Penny Murphy, Bonnie Thiel, Daniel Jones, and Elizabeth Parish, who put up with the ravings of a Vaseline "addict." Thanks also to the friends I've made along the way — especially Marna and Bob Hays.

— Terry Fedosky

TABLE OF CONTENTS

PROLOGUE

The little boy sat in the barber chair and looked into the mirror that ran the whole length of the barber shop. The front mirror reflected the little boy from the front as well as the back by reflecting from another full-length mirror behind him. The many reflections seemed to go on forever.

As the bright Depression-era sunlight streamed into the shop, the barber picked up a yellow-green bottle with a spout top and sprinkled water on the little boy's hair. As the barber shook the bottle, a kaleidoscopic explosion of yellow and green flashes of sunlight reflected back and forth from the front to rear mirrors into infinity.

The little boy's eyes opened with wonder.

"What is that stuff?" he asked the barber.

"Just water," mumbled the barber.

So it had to be the bottle, thought the boy. He looked at the bottle now sitting on the shelf in front of him. The sun shone on it and the glass was yellow, now green, now yellow-green. No doubt it was magic glass, and, strangely, none of the grown-ups in the shop seemed to notice.

The little boy made a silent promise to himself.

"When I grow up, I'm gonna have some of that magic glass. …"

— Jay L. Glickman

INTRODUCTION TO THE ORIGINAL EDITION

It's been called Vaseline, canary, uranium, topaz, yellow, Canaria, Anna Yellow, Lenora Green, and Chameleon. To this day, many dealers and glass collectors are still unsure as to what this attractive yet strange glass is all about.

There is traditionally a distinction drawn between "new" and "old" Vaseline glass. This ranges from the esthetes among us who will accept only "canary" glass as the truly early Vaseline, to the overly generous who call any yellow-green glass "Vaseline type."

Other misconceptions include the notion that Vaseline glass must have a "greasy" feel or appearance, that opalescent Vaseline glass is the variety most likely to have the most value, and that Vaseline glass can still be made in large quantities today.

I've collected Vaseline glass for over 30 years now and I've heard it all. I've heard that only the "old" Vaseline is the real thing and the "reproductions" never are genuine, that the lighter the shade the better, that the darker the shade the better, the greener the better, the yellower the better, and why collect it anyway since it's all dangerously radioactive and it's rarely signed!

This book has been written to cut through the layers of ignorance, misconception, and misinformation that have encrusted this beautiful glass since it was first recognized as a distinctive type of collectible.

Most glass books are written about glass made by a certain craftsman or company of a certain period or method of manufacture.

This book cuts through all lines and is about a color variation—but what a color!

… And it is more than a color; it is a distinctive, separate, and verifiable type of glass!

— Jay L. Glickman

INTRODUCTION TO THE REVISED EDITION

The first time I heard the term "Vaseline glass," I was admiring a piece at a yard sale. I took it home with me, little knowing I was about to begin a great adventure. Amazingly, I already had a few pieces of Vaseline glass, dating back to my days as a demonstrator in the seventies for Wheatonware, a subsidiary of Wheaton Glass. We just didn't call it Vaseline!

The search for information is almost as interesting as the hunt for the glass itself. I was ecstatic when I discovered Jay's book, "Yellow - Green Vaseline!"

For the most part, I've tried to show patterns or pieces that didn't appear in the original book. Several of these are not identified as to the manufacturer. Hopefully, someone else will recognize them and enlighten me. I've also provided corrections to the original text, as new information has come to light since this book was published in 1991.

Collecting Vaseline glass has been a continuous learning experience. Only another collector can imagine the thrill of leafing through a book or catalogue and spotting a piece from one's personal collection. Maybe you will be the one to discover something helpful in identifying a piece that has puzzled you. I hope so!

—Terry Fedosky

1. YELLOW-GREEN VASELINE!
A RIDDLE WRAPPED IN AN ENIGMA

Even its accepted name is a misconception and a misnomer.

First of all, the term "Vaseline glass" is a relatively new label. Before the 1930s there is no record of the name "Vaseline" having been applied to glass. This fact was confirmed in a conversation I had with Frank Fenton, retired chairman of the board of the Fenton Art Glass Company.

According to Mr. Fenton, "Vaseline" was being used by antique dealers in the mid-1930s, but no one knows whether a dealer or collector first coined the term. Mr. Fenton is fairly certain that glass manufacturers did not use the term "Vaseline" before 1937. That year, and again in 1938, the Fenton Art Glass Company produced some Daisy and Button pieces. One of the available colors was Vaseline.

Mr. Fenton recalled that uranium and its compounds were unavailable for civilian use from shortly after Pearl Harbor until the Atomic Energy Commission eased restrictions on their use in 1951. When uranium-bearing chemicals were again allowed to flow into the civilian market, the yellow-green glass that was so popular in Victorian times began to reappear.

Dealers saw the need for a label and Vaseline was the obvious choice because of the color similarity to the lubricant of the same name. Some dealers and collectors were influenced by the new term and began to think of the glass as having oily or greasy characteristics—a total misconception.

Every manufacturer had its own name for this glass. In its early days it was called simply yellow or canary glass—a misnomer again since the glass is more than just yellow. Interestingly enough, the early uranium oxides added to a lead glass formula did produce a more yellow glass, but this yellow color cannot be used as a test of age, for these same manufacturers did not have any quality controls. The author owns many early examples of yellow-green glass that came about because of traces of iron impurities in the sand used.

Although the "canary" term has survived to this day, it really cannot be used to differentiate "old" Vaseline glass, i.e. pre-1941, from "new." For reasons that I will outline later in this book, there is no reason to make such a distinction.

Many museum directors argue that the term used in England, "uranium glass," should be the right name. My opinion of this is that it is too all-inclusive. It can be argued that custard glass and Burmese glass also come under the heading of uranium glass since they contain uranium sulfite and/or uranium sulfides as coloring agents. The difference, of course, is that while custard and Burmese glass are translucent or opaque, Vaseline glass is yellow-green and transparent.

So therefore all transparent yellow-green glass is Vaseline glass? Wrong!

Many dealers and collectors still believe that if you hold a "real" piece of Vaseline glass up to the sun you will see two colors, yellow and green, and if not, it is not the real thing. Wrong! The author owns at least a dozen yellow-green pieces of glass that will flash both colors in sunlight and still are not Vaseline glass.

In recent times in particular, but often in the past, many dealers sold and many collectors bought yellow-green glass that was not Vaseline. This is because glass manufacturers knew that the proper blending of non-uranium coloring agents can product the appearance of Vaseline glass in order to bypass the current legal restrictions and high cost of making the real thing.

In spite of all these apparent dead ends as to what is the real thing, Vaseline glass remains the most verifiable of glass and the easiest to prove!

2. THE ULTRA-VIOLET FACTOR

Since most of the lectures that I give on Vaseline glass to antique and glass clubs occur in the evening, I ask my audience to take my word for it that Vaseline glass flashes two colors in the sunlight. Just as their eyes glaze over, and they think they are looking at just another variety of glass, I turn off the lights and shine a portable ultraviolet light on various pieces of Vaseline glass scattered around the room. The beautiful yellow-green glows never fail to get the audience's full attention and admiration.

Ultraviolet is the key factor in the identification of Vaseline glass. This light, often called "black light," emits high energy emissions of electrons. In the case of Vaseline glass, which usually contains about 2% uranium oxide, the light's strong flow of electrons has an unsettling effect on the relatively unstable uranium atom. The electrons circling the nucleus of the atom are pulled out of the orbit towards the ultraviolet light and back to the nucleus again. Resulting energy is in the form of yellow-green light characteristic of uranium.

This yellow-green glow is characteristic of uranium-bearing glass and will also occur with custard and Burmese glass. The latter two glasses, however, are easily distinguished from Vaseline in that they are not transparent, and Vaseline glass is. Moreover, any other yellow-green glass—such as those containing ferrous, chromium or sulphur compounds—will not fluoresce or glow under ultraviolet.

Clear glass containing manganese fluoresces under ultraviolet light, but not with the same intensity as uranium-bearing Vaseline glass. (Manganese was added to the batch as a decolorizing agent to neutralize iron impurities in the sand.) The bright glow from Vaseline glass is unmistakable, making this glass easy to verify.

Other types of glass are more difficult to verify. Collectors of red glass may wonder if a given piece contains gold as a coloring agent. There are cheaper substitutes for gold, such as selenium, which will produce red and off-red colors. This question also interests Vaseline glass collectors, since Vaseline and ruby glass sometimes appear in combination on pieces by Northwood and Jefferson.

Mr. Frank Fenton states: "It has not been my experience that you can get the true cranberry color without gold." He does acknowledge that shades of red can be produced with selenium. The same applies to the use of manganese compounds in the manufacture of antique amethyst glass. After looking at these imitation reds, pinks, and purples, even the "experts" are stumped as to which are the "real" rubies, cranberries, and amethysts.

Not so with Vaseline glass! No "experts" are needed—just an ultraviolet light and, thanks to the uranium in the glass, a beautiful yellow-green glow for identification and confirmation of true Vaseline glass.

Until a few years ago, ultraviolet lights were bulky and heavy, unlike the battery-operated black lights that can be taken to shows, auctions, and sales for on-site verification.

One warning in regard to ultraviolet light: Only long-wave ultraviolet can be used. Short-wave ultraviolet can cause permanent retinal damage to the eye, and it really doesn't do the job any better.

Be that as it may, ultraviolet light makes our definition of Vaseline glass complete. VASELINE GLASS IS A TRANSPARENT YELLOW-GREEN GLASS WHICH FLUORESCES UNDER ULTRAVIOLET LIGHT!

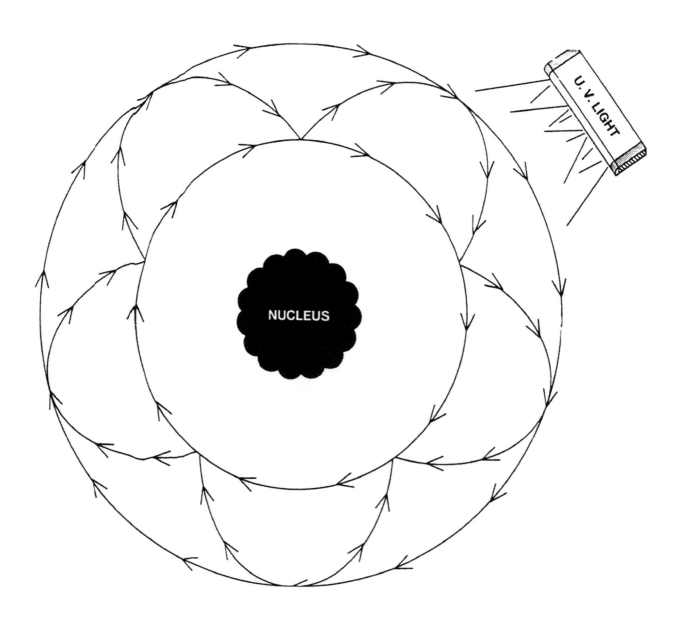

Uranium atom electrons being attracted back and forth between
the nucleus of the uranium atom and ultraviolet light.

3. THE GENIE IN THE YELLOW-GREEN BOTTLE

For the span of approximately 100 years between the middle of the 19th and 20th centuries, uranium in the form of uranium dioxide was looked upon merely as an attractive coloring agent. It was used as a dye for glass, paints, and, to a small extent, textiles. It was used to achieve a rich yellow color, and it was noted that in higher concentrations a greenish hue was added. The dye seemed also to give a brilliance and brightness when it was added. Surprisingly, in the past and to this day, uranium compounds have been used as brightening agents in dentures.

With the advent of the Nuclear Age in 1945, uranium lost its placid reputation and became synonymous with harmful radiation. Happily, this does not apply to Vaseline glass.

First of all, the coloring agent used in glass is not the unstable and radioactive element uranium, but the more stable compound uranium dioxide. Secondly, this uranium compound is only 1% to 2% per volume of the glass. Finally, and most importantly, it is the medium, glass itself, which contributes to the safety of Vaseline glass.

Although regarded physically as a supercooled liquid rather than a true solid, glass provides an effective barrier or shield to radiation. Glass is actually used in radiation rooms for such purposes.

There are four types of emissions from uranium and its compounds, all of which are radioactive. They are alpha, beta, and gamma rays and radon gas. Testing Vaseline glass with a Geiger counter yields very low readings for alpha and beta radiation. For such emissions the genie is safely locked in. This leaves gamma radiation emission as the remaining factor to contend with. Fortunately, since gamma radiation is extremely short range, it dissipates almost immediately.

In order to take the radioactive pulse of Vaseline glass and thereby test its safety, the author in conjunction with Dr. Brian Redmond of Wilkes College, an expert on uranium and its emissions, used a gamma scintillator to record gamma ray emission. Putting the scintillator about 15 feet away from a collection of about 700 pieces of Vaseline glass, the instrument recorded .09 microroentgens per hour, which is the same as normal background radiation indoors or outdoors. From 10 feet away the reading rose to .15 microroentgens per hour, and from 7 feet away to .22 microroentgens per hour. Next, we piled approximately 50 pieces of Vaseline glass around, under, and on top of the scintillator. The reading at pointblank range was still .22 microroentgens per hour.

A few months later, to my surprise, I discovered from Mr. Frank Fenton that the Fenton Art Glass Company had done similar tests with a team of scientists and had gotten similar results. Mr. Fenton stated that "before the batch for Vaseline glass is melted, it is dangerous. Once it is melted, whether molten or cold, it is then not dangerous."

Finally, we left a radon detector in each of three cabinets jammed with Vaseline glass for the prescribed period of six days. Each detector tested out at .07, an extremely low reading and far from the human danger point of 4.0.

The bottom line is that there is an insignificant amount of radiation emission from Vaseline glass roughly equivalent in distance to source as TV and microwave-oven emissions. What a small price to pay for having such beauty in color, shape, and light form!

4. EARLY STARTS AND STOPS

The history of Vaseline glass is a chronicle of false starts based on cyclical searches for a yellow dye at a given time and the availability of uranium ore in a given place.

The earliest evidence of uranium, i.e. Vaseline, glass was discovered in a colored-glass mosaic excavated from an imperial Roman villa on Cape Posilipo on the Bay of Naples by R.T. Gunther of Oxford University. He dated the pieces back to 79 A.D., and under analysis they were found to contain a little over 1% of an oxide of uranium, about the same percentage per volume that would be used in years to come. According to historian Earle R. Caley, the date 79 A.D. "may be taken as fixing the approximate time of the first use of any kind of a material containing uranium."

Unfortunately, no more uranium-bearing glass was found in other Roman excavations due to the expanded use of easily available ferric oxide by the Romans. Obviously, the sample of uranium glass was the result of active trade which Rome conducted with North Africa, where outcroppings of uranium ore are found in a yellow-green state.

Throughout the medieval times the use of uranium in glass was nonexistent because uranium ore was not available in Europe in a yellow-green state, but rather in pitchblende, a black ore. Medieval yellow glass, which was used in stained-glass windows, was made from silver compounds.

In the 17th and 18th centuries, the Chinese experimented in achieving readily available yellow dyes to portray the imperial color. They stumbled on the use of uranium in glass jewelry, but did not continue the effort due to the presence of more common substitutes.

The breakthrough finally came in 1789 in Germany. A poor druggist named Martin Heinrich Klaproth was experimenting with pitchblende, a rather common black ore then thought to be a blend of iron and zinc. He dissolved some pitchblende in nitric acid and then neutralized the acid with potash. A yellow precipitate emerged. Klaproth concluded that the yellow substance was a new element and named it after the newly discovered planet Uranus. It wasn't until 1841 that a French scientist, Eugene Melchior Peligot, showed that the "element" obtained by Klaproth was actually uranium dioxide and not uranium.

At last the components fell into place. There was an available ore as well as the technology to extract the desired yellow dye. Also available was the newly invented glass press in America. The dawning of the Victorian Era was at hand.

The discovery of the new yellow material could not have occurred at a more opportune time. It was midway into the 19th century, and throughout the world there was an acceleration of the Industrial Revolution which had started earlier in the century and which combined newly discovered techniques and chemicals. Clear glass, which had been individually painted and engraved at great cost, now gave way to new colored glass which could be mass produced.

Among these new colored glasses was uranium glass, or, as it was called in America, canary, and later, Vaseline glass.

5. THE BEGINNING

The fortunate coincidence of the perfection of the process of isolating uranium dioxide from pitchblende in 1841 together with the development of the glass press in the 1830s gave rise to the first commercial use of uranium in glass in the 1850s. The primitive method of blowing glass into a mold was used less frequently as the use of the glass press increased.

The very first pieces made of Vaseline glass from pitchblende ore occurred in Bohemia on a small scale, as will be explained in Chapter 11. Although the credit for the first large-scale commercial production of uranium glass is generally attributed to the firm of Lloyd and Summerfield of Birmingham, England, in 1857, this is not true in the author's opinion. Indications are that the prize for large-scale production must go to the Boston and Sandwich Glass Company, which in the 1840s made canary glass items such as whale-oil lamps and, later, the Dolphin and other early candlesticks.

The author has in his possession an early American (possibly Sandwich) lady's mucilage pot in canary which is dated 1840. With the notable exception of lacy glass, however, very little mass-produced canary glass was made until about 1850.

Before 1850 the early methods of processing and the lack of efficient temperature control often resulted in dull and cloudy glassware. To minimize this flaw the early glass companies of the 1830s and 40s designed stippled patterns with raised dots, which also increased the refractive qualities of the glass. This bit of Yankee ingenuity converted many an ugly duckling batch of glass into beautiful, though inexpensive, lacy glass tableware. By the 1850s, better glass recipes and pressing techniques did away with the need for stippling, and the ideal became the imitation of cut crystal.

Then, as now, members of management and labor switched sides and loyalties from one glass company to another, carrying with them secret recipes, pattern secrets, and sources of supply. As there were few catalogs available before 1850, it is almost impossible to tell which of the early glass companies made any given item. Some glass experts have tried to make order of this chaos by determining the origin of glass shards found at early factory sites. This piecing together is quite academic, however, since the companies were constantly imitating each other's patterns and ideas.

At this point a word to the wise collector should be sufficient. The term "Sandwich glass" is used much too liberally by so-called experts and hopeful dealers. In many cases, there is no way of being absolutely sure that a piece of canary glass, flint though it may be, was manufactured by the Boston and Sandwich Glass Company. It could be New England Glass Company, or Bakewell, Pears and Company of Pittsburgh, or possibly even McKee.

In addition, the so-called canary glass can sometimes be yellow-green even though it is a flint glass. This is due to the fact that early glassmaking was sorely lacking in quality control, and iron impurities in the sand could often give the coloration a more yellow-green tint than is usually common in canary. The only real difference between some canary glass and Vaseline is that the base for the former is a lead glass, and for the latter a lime or soda-ash glass. In the case of impurities in canary, it is really impossible to tell one from the other except possibly by slight differences in weight.

Be that as it may, all early American pressed glass had one common ingredient, it contained lead. Although its beauty is unquestioned, this comparatively expensive feature contained the seed of the demise of the early glass companies.

6. LEAD TO LIME

By the 1860s, a proliferation of new glass companies ensued, with resulting high competition and depressed prices. The need for close-by cheap coal to fuel glass furnaces resulted in some new glass companies in the Pittsburgh area. In addition, the discovery of natural gas deposits in Ohio and West Virginia led other new glass companies to locate even further west. Such new companies as Adams, Atterbury, Crystal, Doyle, O'Hara, and Campbell, Jones located in the Pittsburgh area in the 1860s, and such companies as Central, Bellaire Goblet, Belmont, and Hobbs, Brockunier set up shop in Ohio and West Virginia.

In 1863, a superintendent at the New England Glass Company named William Leighton, Sr. quit the pioneer company, where his father had also been employed, to become a partner and superintendent at Hobbs, Brockunier and Company of Wheeling, West Virginia. This event may appear trivial, but in reality it was to change the entire American glass industry.

William Leighton had grown up in the glass industry and was highly skilled in the formulation of coloring agents. Among his inventions was an original formula for ruby glass. He also experimented with production of a cheaper form of glass. At Hobbs, Brockunier in 1864, his experiments led him to substitute bicarbonate of soda for the carbonate of soda (soda ash) that was previously used. The result was a soda-lime glass that was suitable for pressing and nearly as brilliant as the more expensive lead glass.

The cheaper new glass immediately spread to other companies and gave rise to new ones. The early eastern glass companies could not endure the competition and either went under, changed their operation to the higher profit margin and lower production of "art" and flint glass for the carriage trade, or else adopted the new soda-lime glass.

Leighton's former employers at the New England Glass Company chose to continue manufacturing the high quality, more expensive flint glass. Their logic was based on the fact that it was clear glass rather than colored glass that was in demand. They felt, with some justification, that the clear flint glass was brighter and heavier and therefore had more in common with the brilliant cut lead glass which it sought to emulate. The staid old glass company was certain that people would pay more for the quality flint glass, and for awhile it was right. But labor and fuel problems eventually prompted a move to Toledo, Ohio, in 1888, where the business was renamed the Libbey Glass Company.

William Leighton, Sr. resigned from Hobbs, Brockunier in 1869 and returned to New England. His son, William Jr., took over his father's position in the firm. Although pressed wares continued in production using the new formula, Hobbs, Brockunier also produced blown wares including art glass and cut glass. In 1884, the younger Leighton patented an art glass called "spangled glass" which featured tiny mica flakes embedded between layers of glass.

The die was cast, however, for the mass market. The newly emerging middle class called for less expensive pressed glass, which relegated quality low-production flint and art glass to an ever-shrinking position in the industry.

7. Vaseline Pattern Glass

With the advent of the glass press and the larger-scale production it allowed, glass patterns were limited, first, by the types of patterns popular in cut glass and, second, by the relatively low number of glass companies.

Now that less expensive soda-lime glass was made available by literally hundreds of glass companies, the amount and variety of patterns suddenly became endless in scope. The patterns, along with variations in color, were a major means of competition, competition made even more fierce when the deciding factor in survival was price.

The principle of the day was the higher the production, the lower the cost, and, therefore, the lower the price. The new glass companies springing up were usually housed in hastily built wooden buildings, and fires from the constantly burning furnaces were quite common.

Quality control was limited, and batches differed in quality and quantity of ingredients. Although clear glass was most in demand and highest in production, it was also the type to suffer most from mass production. The clear glass was often off-color, dingy, and full of imperfections.

Glass companies began to develop more intricate patterns to hide these imperfections and devoted more of their production to colored glass to hide the off-color present in the clear variety. While less than one-third of all patterns featured colors, by far most of the colors that were featured were greens, blues, and ambers. The color which we call Vaseline was made in smaller quantities and in fewer patterns. This is reflected today in the scarcity of Vaseline glass—even those pieces from Vaseline's most popular period, the Victorian Era.

Mr. Frank Fenton told the author the reason for this limited production of Vaseline glass in no uncertain terms. Mr. Fenton was told by his father, and later found out for himself, that Vaseline glass sold well on the first issuance of any pattern, but then sold poorly on reissues. Unless production was strictly controlled, the result would be an abnormally high inventory. This was recognized throughout the industry, and it explains why most glass companies never made Vaseline glass at all. The reason for this phenomenon will be explained in later chapters.

8. NON-OPALESCENT PATTERNS IN VASELINE

Primitive free-blown glass was devoid of pattern until the advent of mold-blown glass. At first, the wooden molds used were incised with simple patterns such as panel, flute, tulip, or spiral. As more durable metal molds became standard, the patterns became more complex with such adaptations as thumbprint, diamond, prism, and drape, by themselves and in combination.

The purpose in patterning mass-produced glass was two-fold: first, to hide the inevitable production flaws, and, second, to enhance marketability by emulating the beautiful and expensive cut glass of the American Brilliant Period in sets of tableware entailing dozens of pieces.

In Vaseline glass, the most successful of the patterns by far was Daisy and Button. This pattern was copied from the cut-glass "Russian" design patented by Hawkes in 1882. The complex faceted surface of this pattern reflects and flashes light from all angles, which in the Vaseline color is extremely attractive.

Within a short period after its introduction, Daisy and Button and all its variations were being pressed in Vaseline by at least six different companies. By the 20th century, there was hardly a glass company that had not pressed Daisy and Button in one form or another in tableware, toothpick holders, clocks, shoes, whimsies, inkwells, banquet pieces, pickle casters, and caster sets.

Of the thousands of glass patterns, it is impossible to know just how many were pressed in the canary or Vaseline color. In the first edition of this book, the author estimated this number at about 55 patterns pressed (not including opalescent Vaseline). This figure was based on more than 30 years of experience as a collector. Of these, approximately 30 patterns were pressed in quantities sufficiently large not to be termed as rare. Bear in mind that some companies merely had test pressings in Vaseline, and these may constitute a real find for the collector. On the other hand, certain patterns were not originally pressed in Vaseline, and because the molds had not been destroyed, they were reproduced at a later time. Such reproductions will be referred to later in this book.

Patterns Pressed in Canary/Vaseline (Non-Opalescent)

Austrian	Medallion
*Basketweave	Panel and Star (Column Block)
Cane and variations	Pressed Diamond
Cathedral	Ranson
Dahlia	Rose in Snow
*Daisy and Button and variations	Rose Sprig
Deer and Pine Tree	Scalloped Tape (Jewel Band)
Dewey	Spirea Band (Square and Dot)
*Diamond Quilted	Star and Punty
Fine Cut and variation	Thousand Eye
Frosted Block	Three Panel
*Hobnail and variation	Tree of Life
Honeycomb	Two Panel

*Inverted Thumbprint (Argus)	*Wildflower
*Maple Leaf	Willow Oak

*Reproductions in some pieces

These are the patterns one is most apt to find today in canary/Vaseline. Since there are many fine pattern glass books on the market, it is not the author's intent to merely repeat their information, but to point out which patterns are of interest to the Vaseline glass collector.

For the record there are a few patterns which were originally listed in their original sales literature as being available in yellow or canary, but which are either rare or really non-existent except for isolated pieces or prototypes. They are:

Barred Forget-Me-Not	Hummingbird
Beaded Flange	Jacob's Ladder
Cupid and Venus	Log Cabin
Double Beetle Band	Monkey
Draped Fan	Paneled Diamond with Fan
Grasshopper with Insect	Pleat and Panel
Harvard	Ringed Framed Ovals
Hour Glass	Wheat and Barley

At the time the first edition of this book appeared, Wallace-Homestead published Bill Jenks and Jerry Luna's *Early American Pattern Glass 1850-1910*. Unlike most pattern glass references, Jenks and Luna listed the color production for each of the nearly 400 patterns in their book. In addition to patterns on the lists above, these authors identified an additional 16 patterns that they believe included pieces in Vaseline glass:

Adonis	Jersey Swirl
Amazon	Primrose
Ashburton	Queen
Diamond Point	Raindrop
Diamond Thumbprint	Swan
Hanover	Valencia Waffle
Hartley	Waffle and Thumbprint
Horn of Plenty	Wooden Pail

It is likely that Vaseline glass was made in other patterns as well. Compared to the total number of pressed glass patterns (5,000 by one estimate), the total is still quite small—probably less than 100.

It is important to remember that the primary use of pattern from a merchandising point of view was to help sell tableware in sets and thus increase glass sales and production during the most competitive era in American glass history—the period from 1860 to 1890. Although many Vaseline glass collectors may want to restrict themselves to collecting one pattern, they may be missing out on the fascinating tangential side trips to which a more varied collection will lead.

9. THE VICTORIAN HIGH TIDE

During the height of the popularity of Vaseline glass, roughly from 1860 to 1890, various pieces were made that were not part of tableware sets. The Vaseline-glass color of soft yellow-green seemed to win full acceptance throughout the Victorian home. This, in the author's opinion was not due merely to the dictates of fashion, but also in the interests of color and lighting.

Victorian lighting was almost exclusively by kerosene or gas light, soft light easily absorbed by the prevalent dark wall and floor decor. Under such soft light, the yellow-green of Vaseline glass actually seems to glow to the human eye. This is not flight-of-fancy opinion, but actual scientifically based fact. The frequency of light's wave lengths is crucial to what the human eye sees in examination of a substance bordering on two colors. As will be explained in a later chapter, more efficient lighting in later years sharply affected the future of Vaseline glass.

The human eye can see the entire spectrum in yellow-green, and it is thus the easiest of colors to perceive. Whether indoors or outdoors, as darkness increases, the last color that the eye can see before it is subjected to total darkness is yellow-green. Conversely, yellow-green is the first color the eye sees as we go from dark to light.

No wonder the Victorians loved this glass! In their dimly lit and flickering gaslight environment, Vaseline glass provided one of the few exceptions to a dark and drab setting; whatever sunlight came into the home was picked up by Vaseline glass. Thus, Victorians embraced Vaseline glass as a medium for everything from whimsies to commemorative pieces, from luxurious cut Vaseline glass to elegant banquet pieces, from functional houseware items to quack cure and pseudo-scientific devices.

SHOES, HATS, AND WHIMSIES

The September 2, 1886 issue of *Pottery and Glassware Reporter*, pertaining to the glass production of the firm of George Duncan and Sons, said: ". . . They have a lot of odds and ends here, shoes, hats, parasols, slippers etc. for ornament and use combined. They are employed as the receptacles of various nic-nacs (*sic*) about the house, and can be hung up or placed in suitable positions where they are serviceable, not to speak of their ornate qualities. This firm is running full with both furnaces and trade with them is improving."

The shoes pressed in Vaseline included slippers in various sizes, baby booties, and high-topped shoes. The companies that manufactured them included Duncan, Gillinder, Bryce, Smith, Belmont, Columbia, and possibly Campbell, Jones & Co., either through direct patent or by licensee rights. By far, the most common pattern used was Daisy and Button, although there are some examples of booties in fine cut and some slippers without any pattern at all.

Hats in Vaseline were generally of the top-hat variety in Daisy and Button. There were some flat and porkpie hats pressed earlier, as well as some military hats pressed later, no doubt in response to the Spanish-American War.

Whimsies in Vaseline included open whisk brooms, open bottles, stoves, figural butter dishes, and various animal and bird toothpick holders and mustard jars.

Many of these shoes, hats, whimsies, and toothpick holders were reproduced in the 20th century, to the distress of many glass collectors. When we talk later about the Vaseline variety of these reproductions, however, there is no need for consternation by collectors or dealers who can see the big picture.

VASELINE GLASS EXPOSITION PIECES

In 1888, the Libbey Glass Company was established in Toledo, Ohio, and the new company wasted no time in showing off its cut glass at the Columbian Exposition of 1893 in Chicago. At the fair, Libbey distributed small Vaseline glass souvenirs such as toothpick holders, match safes, and cups and saucers with the company's name and "Columbian Exposition" pressed in the base. Some pieces are dated and thus constitute some of the very few pieces of Vaseline glass that are dated. The Exposition pieces are great finds for collectors.

SPECIAL AND COMMEMORATIVE PLATES

Although most Victorian commemorative and special plates were made of clear glass, there are a few notable exceptions in Vaseline glass, such as the Knights of Labor Plate by Bakewell, Pears and Company (circa 1879), the Maple Leaf Grant Peace Plate by Gillinder and Sons (circa 1888), the Currier and Ives "Balky Mule" Tray by Bellaire Goblet Company (circa 1888), the Columbia Shield Plate and the "Give Us This Day" Bread Plate by U.S. Glass Company (circa 1895), as well as the Basketweave Rural Scene Plate (circa 1885). Indeed, there may be other special or commemorative plates in Vaseline glass out there that could be the results of trial runs or special orders, and lucky the collector who acquires such a treasure!

FUNCTIONAL AND FURNISHING VASELINE PIECES

As referred to earlier in this chapter, the use of Vaseline glass to bring color and light into the Victorian home prompted the manufacture of various items far afield from tableware.

For instance, Vaseline glass tiebacks were made with pewter shanks in floral or geometric designs to hold back curtains or draperies. The Vaseline glass facings of these tiebacks have deep and intricate facetings and designs to pick up and reflect every bit of natural and artificial light available.

These designs and facets are also found on Vaseline glass doorknobs and drawer pulls to bring color and sparkle to a drab Victorian world. Even such mundane items as furniture casters were often made of Vaseline glass, and surprisingly, even though most of these casters were hidden by the massive furniture of the time, they too were intricately detailed.

Mantle clocks encased in Vaseline glass also added color and light to the Victorian home. Strategically placed above the hearth, these clocks reflected the light of the fireplace. The most popular of these clocks was the McKee camelback which has three different patterns to reflect light—Mitre, Daisy and Button, and a floral pattern—all in the same piece. Other Vaseline-encased clocks have set-backs, facets, and hobnails to achieve the same light enhancement. Even the very lamps that shed light on the Victorian home were often made of Vaseline glass, including first whale oil and then kerosene lamps of all sizes.

One of the stranger functional uses of the Victorian Vaseline glass had to do with the mannerisms and atmosphere of the time. It was a time when infectious airborne diseases and air pollution from coal-burning stoves and machines ran rampant—far worse than today in many respects. The proper Victorian lady, unlike her male counterpart, was not expected to spit, but rather to discretely and demurely expectorate into a lady's spittoon which she kept in her muff or purse. These little spittoons were usually made of porcelain, some were made of Vaseline glass and came with or without a handle.

The functional uses of Vaseline glass also extended to apothecary jars, especially to hold contents that would keep better in a colored glass. Their Latin and English descriptive labels, such as "powdered assorted bones" and "oil of dusky rose," are often amusing by our standards.

Complementary to apothecary bottle collecting is the collecting of cologne and perfume bottles. Victorian bottles were larger than the perfume and cologne bottles made after the turn of the century and had more intricate cutting and etchings. The small bottles of Victorian times were used for smelling salts or ammonia, de rigueur for funerals, to revive one from a proper Victorian swoon.

QUACK CURES AND WHIZ-BANGS

The Victorian Era provided a setting for the charlatan and con man living by P.T. Barnum's credo that there's "a sucker born every minute." Licensing was haphazard, and the landscape was littered with "professors" and "doctors" who usually had some "galvanic electrical" device or elixir to cure, not just something, but everything.

The ailing but gullible public allowed themselves to be strapped or wired to strange devices which gave off all kinds of noises and lights. Running electrical charges through gases in colored tubes would usually give the effect of a machine that was doing something amazing. The usual effect of color was heightened if the tubes were of Vaseline glass. For want of a better term, these devices are derisively known as "whiz-bangs."

The fraud didn't stop there. Toward the end of the 19th century radium was discovered, and it was thought that it had curative powers. What better way to dispense a "radium elixir" or "vitalizer" than from a Vaseline glass dispenser? It is no accident that radium and Vaseline glass are both yellow-green, since radium is a "daughter" or descending element resulting from the disintegration of uranium.

BANQUET PIECES

Let us go from the ridiculous to the sublime in the spectrum of Vaseline glass—the banquet pieces.

Although the newly emerging Victorian lower middle class seemed insatiable in its hunger for pattern glass tableware, some astute silverware companies such as Tufts, Meriden, and Reed and Barton saw a market for upgraded glass serving pieces mounted in signed silver-plate holders. This was the upper middle class that found only fine china and "art glass" acceptable.

Vaseline glass serving pieces set in silver holders became a symbol of elegance in Victorian times, even if these pieces spent most of the time in china cabinets. The silver-plate holders were replete with scroll work filigree and with designs entailing geometrics as well as flora and fauna. Some also included the popular Kate Greenaway children.

The Vaseline glass inserts were mostly in the fully accepted Daisy and Button pattern. However, some pieces were Pressed Diamond by the Central Glass Company, and there were even some patterns such as Shell and Tassel and Crossed Block which usually weren't made in Vaseline except for banquet-piece inserts.

For the most part these banquet pieces consisted of bowls, caster sets, and vertical celery holders. Also popular were boat-shaped mounted bowls called Cenestas (named after one of the Vanderbilt yachts). These bowls today are erroneously called canoe bowls. Upwardly mobile Victorians bought them because they were yacht related. It would never do to keep a mere canoe in one's china cabinet!

By far the most popular of the banquet pieces was the typically Victorian pickle caster. Ostensibly, it was a table piece used for serving pickles, and it often came with silver-plated tongs hanging on the holder. According to the repeated interviews with people who inherited these pieces, the pickle caster was rarely used for the purpose for which it was designed. Rather, it was expected that every proper Victorian family have one in its china cabinet. Judging from the inscriptions that many pickle casters have on their lids, it appears that they were commonly given as gifts.

CUT VASELINE GLASS

The rarest type of Vaseline glass, and probably the most beautiful, is cut Vaseline. It is extremely rare today because of the very small quantities which were made. Manufacturers were reluctant to produce a type of glass which was more costly and, surprisingly enough, unpopular.

Only the rich could afford the luxury of cut glass, but more importantly, within that limited cut-glass market itself, the demand was for clear crystal. Clarity and heavy faceting to achieve the ultimate in light refraction were the goals in cut-glass manufacturing, and rainbow-like refractions could only be achieved with clear crystal.

The author has interviewed former glasscutters and some of their surviving kin who cut for Dorflinger and Hawkes. None of the people interviewed had ever cut Vaseline blanks or even heard of it being cut. They all testified that cut clear crystal was all that was cut or in demand.

However, some Vaseline glass was cut on special order, mostly for European wine decanters and cologne bottles. Cut Vaseline glass breaks down light into flashes of yellow and green, and, although breathtakingly beautiful, it cannot bring you the rainbow of colors that crystal cut glass delivers.

BLOWN VASELINE GLASS

Scarce though it may be, blown Vaseline glass was produced, mostly on special order. The author owns several blown pieces, including one dated as recently as 1982.

It was economics which determined that blown Vaseline glass was made in small amounts. Expensive free-blown or mold-blown glass was priced out of the market by pressed glass through most of the Victorian Era as well as the post-Victorian years.

In the first edition of this book, the author expressed concern about the health hazards of blowing Vaseline glass. It came as a relief to learn from Frank Fenton that these fears were largely unfounded. Uranium must be handled with care when mixed in the batch, but this glass is not dangerous once it reaches the molten state. This point is further clarified in Chapter 3.

By the 1890s, the high tide of Victorian Vaseline glass production had passed its zenith, and never again would the public see such huge amounts and varieties of this beautiful glass.

10. OPALESCENT VASELINE GLASS

The last decade of the 19th century saw the new rising market of a growing middle class. Its demand was not for utilitarian tableware, but for decorative pieces using more exotic and interesting variations of glass. This gave rise to a category known today as "art glass," and the earliest and one of the most popular members of this group was opalescent glass.

Several new glass companies such as Northwood, Beaumont, Jefferson, and Fenton utilized the same colors, including Vaseline, as previously used in pattern glass, but with patterns for opalescent glass. In addition, the pieces pressed in opalescent glass were for the most part not complete tableware sets, but elaborate vases, compotes, cruets, water sets, and epergnes.

Although in earlier days some mold-blown opalescent glass was produced, it was a time-consuming and expensive process. However, in 1886, the irrepressible William Leighton patented a process for pressing opalescent glass by adding bone ash and heat sensitive arsenic to the batch. After pressing, the glass objects were reheated ("warming in") at an auxiliary furnace called a glory hole. This process developed the opalescent edges or rims so prevalent in many articles. Mass production of opalescent glass was now possible.

Although Vaseline was one of the colors pressed, it was made in much smaller quantities than were the other colors, such as clear, blue, and cranberry. As will be outlined later, Vaseline was already becoming an unpopular and old-fashioned color by the 1890s and early 20th century.

Less than half of all opalescent patterns were pressed in Vaseline. They are, along with the manufacturer(s) to press the pattern, as follows:

Alaska—Northwood
Beaded Cable—Northwood
Beaded Shell—National/Duncan
Beatty's Ribbed Opalescent—Beatty
Beatty's Swirl—Beatty
Button Panels—Dugan
Dew Drop—LaBelle
Diamond Point—Northwood
Diamond Spearhead—Northwood/Dugan
Drapery—Northwood (rare in Vaseline)
Everglades (Carnelian)—Northwood
Fan—Dugan

Flora—Beaumont
Fluted Scrolls (Klondyke)—Northwood, Dugan
Iris and Meander—Jefferson
Hobnail—Hobbs/Northwood/Fenton
Meander—Jefferson
Ribbed Basket (Ribbed Spiral)— Model Flint
Shell and Wreath (Manila)—Model Flint
Spanish Lace (mold blown)—Fenton and Northwood
Twist—Model Flint

SELECTED OPALESCENT VASELINE PIECES

Corn Vase—Northwood and Dugan

Dolphin Compote—Northwood/National

Pump and Trough—Northwood

Tree Trunk Vase—Northwood

From a study of William Heacock's *Encyclopedia of Victorian Colored Pattern Glass, Book II, Opalescent Glass from A to Z* and other sources, most published since the first edition of this book, the list can be expanded to include the following opalescent patterns made in Vaseline. As indicated, some were mold blown, not pressed.

Argonaut Shell (Nautilus)—Northwood/Dugan

Cactus—Fenton

Coin Dot (mold blown)—Fenton

Coin Spot (mold blown)—Northwood/Dugan/Hobbs/Fenton

Daffodil—Northwood

Diadem (Sunburst on Shield)—Northwood

Diamond Lace—Fenton

Diamond Stem—Model Flint

Duchess—Riverside

Frosted Leaf and Basketweave—Northwood

Grape and Cable—Northwood

Inverted Fan and Feather—Northwood/Dugan

Inside Ribbing—Beaumont

Intaglio—Northwood

Jackson—Northwood

Jewel and Flower (Encore)—Northwood

Lattice Thumbprint—Central

Opal Open—Northwood

Opal Swirl (mold blown)—Hobbs

Palm Beach—United States Glass

Pressed Diamond (No. 775)—Central

Reverse Swirl (mold blown)—Model Flint

Scroll with Acanthus—Northwood

Spanish Lace (mold blown)—Dugan

Swag with Brackets—Jefferson

Trailing Vine—Coudersport

Wreath and Shell—Model Flint

As stated, the collector will find far fewer pieces per pattern in opalescent Vaseline as opposed to the great variety of tableware pieces available in the non-opalescent Vaseline patterns. Nevertheless, there have been more repeats and reproductions made in opalescent Vaseline than in non-opalescent varieties. The L.G. Wright Company alone issued Vaseline opalescent pieces in the mid-1960s in the following patterns: Rib, Fern, Strawberry and Current, Daisy and Button, Jersey Swirl, Rose Sprig, Moon and Star, Wildflower, and Cherry. Yet many dealers falsely insist that opalescent Vaseline is rarer and more collectible than non-opalescent Vaseline.

There are some beautiful examples of opalescent Vaseline which reflect a high degree of skillful glassmaking, but the fact remains that the addition of a non-reflective opaque ingredient, as used in opalescent Vaseline, cuts down on the colorful, refractive, and fluorescent qualities inherent in clear Vaseline glass.

11. Vaseline + A Change of Scene = Uranium Glass

Vaseline glass evolved differently and at a slower pace outside the United States. From the start, the overall generic term used was "uranium glass." In the United States the color was used to describe the glass; in Europe the coloring ingredient, uranium, was used to identify it. The Europeans don't seem to care that their descriptive term is too all-inclusive. Both custard glass and Burmese glass could be included as being uranium glass since both contain uranium-compound coloring agents. When the Europeans say uranium glass, they mean Vaseline glass.

As stated earlier, the first separation of uranium from a common ore, pitchblende, was done in Germany in 1789 by Martin Klaproth. The pitchblende used originated in the mountains of Bohemia, now known as the Czech Republic and Slovakia. It is therefore no wonder that the use of uranium oxide as a coloring agent for glass first occurred in Bohemia. The glassmaker given credit for this was a Czech named Josef Riedel. The use of uranium oxide in glassmaking before 1840 was directly attributable to him.

It was an expensive process to extract uranium from pitchblende by the Klaproth method, and the uranium salts released sometimes tended to yield greenish glass and sometimes a yellowish glass, depending on the heat applied and the impurities present. Riedel saw the opportunity to change these liabilities into assets. He promptly named the two colors after his wife, calling one Annagruen (green) and the other Annagelb (yellow).

These two glasses made in small quantities were used strictly for presentation pieces to royalty and political figures. The high cost of the uranium dyes obtained from the slow and cumbersome Klaproth method made the cost of uranium glass prohibitive at that time.

Larger scale industrial production of uranium glass began in the 1850s when more efficient methods were developed. Unlike glass manufacturers in America and England, the Bohemians varied their uranium glass through experimentation with the ingredients. Selenium was added to achieve pink uranium glass and sulphur and cadmium to achieve orange and amber uranium glass, respectively. Again, the glass was made into decorative pieces, unlike in America where the emphasis was on tableware.

The pieces were usually hand painted and gilded and uranium glass was also used as a plating or flashing over clear glass. However, by far the greatest amount of Bohemian uranium glass was used for the production of glass rods as raw material in the costume jewelry industry. This glass was referred to in Europe as "chameleon."

Right up to World War II, the Czech glass industry turned out uranium glass items such as toilet sets, ashtrays, paperweights, and doorknobs. All this ceased after World War II, right on up to the 1970s. By that time, the clever Czechs had found yellow-green substitutes for the uranium cut off from them in the post-war years. Collectors would be well advised to test all Czech yellow-green glass with ultraviolet light.

Meanwhile in England and France the use of uranium glass proceeded at a much slower pace. In both countries, cheap available crockery ruled out the extensive use of glass in tableware, and the popularity and production of uranium glass did not approach that of the United States.

According to British records, the first commercial uranium glass produced in England was in 1857 by Lloyd and Summerfield of Birmingham. Other English glass companies, such as Webb, Hammond, and Stevens and Williams, followed suit. In 1889 Thomas Davidson of George Davidson Ltd. patented a process allowing for a creamier shaded opalescence in which glass pieces remain clear at the bottom with opalescence occurring at the top. This process was so successful that England exported this new opalescent glass to the United States and then licensed the process to American glass companies. In England, production of opalescent uranium glass far outstripped production of the non-opalescent before the color fell out of fashion in the early 20th century.

In France, uranium glass was not so much a fashionable or popular color as it was utilitarian. Uranium glass was used in the manufacture of apothecary jars, medicine bottles, and even seltzer bottles in the belief that the color protected the contents. Some French decorative uranium glass by companies such as Vallerysthal was, however, made for export.

12. THE GLASS BUBBLE SHATTERS

In the United States, the early 1890s saw a gradual change in demand for glass in general and for Vaseline glass in particular. The change resulted from several causes that seemed to converge at the same time.

After three decades of steady demand for pattern glass as tableware, the market for these products went into a decline. Throughout the 1890s in issue after issue of the *Crockery and Glass Journal*, the leading industry periodical, there can be found signs of the beginning of the end.

In several issues one finds articles describing the drop in demand for glass in favor of crockery. There are articles describing in detail the lack of demand for "old-fashioned colors" in favor of "decorated crystal." There is even a housewife's comment that she "could never serve food on yellow glass."

There are also articles on how overproduction caused a glut and ensuing lower prices and, ominously, an increase in glass company failures during the depression of 1892-93. Other problems during this period included labor conflicts and the depletion of natural glass. Competition for the surviving factories was intense.

To cope with these difficulties, 18 active glass factories joined together to form the United States Glass Company in 1891. One of its purposes was to reissue the best-selling patterns of the member factories in hopes of reviving demand. Of more than 300 patterns inherited and made by U.S. Glass, only 26 featured Vaseline glass. When these few did not sell, the only ones retained in Vaseline were the Daisy and Button varieties.

About 1900, 19 of the remaining independent firms amalgamated to form the National Glass Company. By 1904, its rank had shrunk through closures and losses from fires.

13. THE DECLINE OF VASELINE 1900-1941

I have been collecting pieces of Vaseline glass obtained from many sources for more than 30 years. Almost every time I had occasion to buy a piece from an estate or from private sources it was something that had been "packed away" and referred to as "that yellow glass."

I remember buying a pair of candlesticks from an elderly lady in the Midwest who told me that she might have more of "that ugly yellow glass packed away someplace" where her mother had put it. She told me her mother had put it away because the yellow was an eyesore and didn't go with anything in the house. Her mother had inherited the glass from her grandmother, and she could never understand why the "old timers" ever liked that yellow glass.

I have heard enough of these stories to know that the decline of Vaseline glass in popularity was not merely due to the dictates of fashion. After all, how could a glass that was so acceptable in one era be so rejected a few years later? Even the people who prized Vaseline glass in tableware and home furnishings through the Victorian Era into the early 1900s probably never understood why their attitude toward this glass changed.

Look at Vaseline glass under sunlight, gaslight, or candlelight, and then look at the same glass under incandescent light or fluorescent light and you will have the answer. Gaslight and candlelight have varying light frequencies observable as slight flickerings to the human eye's scotopic or dark-adapted vision. The human eye's photopic or bright-adapted vision cannot pick up the varying light frequencies of the sun, but they are still there. On the other hand, modern incandescent and fluorescent light are both characterized by a steady, almost unvarying light frequency.

All the colors in the spectrum visible to the human eye also have varying frequencies characteristic of each color. These light frequencies are called nanometers. As seen in the following table, yellow-green is in the exact center of the visible spectrum seen by the human eye.

COLOR	APPROX. FREQUENCY IN NANOMETERS (nm.)
Red	780 - 622
Orange	622 - 597
Yellow	897 - 577
Yellow-Green	577 color of uranium atom
Green	577 - 492
Blue	492 - 455
Violet	455 - 390

The low, fluctuating frequencies of light emitted by the incandescent and/or fluorescent light bulb on Vaseline glass never varies from the yellow range as the human eye perceives it. On the contrary, the fluctuating light frequencies of the sun, gaslight, and candlelight move from the yellow to green range and back again.

To move from the scientific to the romantic, when the observer looks at Vaseline glass under sunlight, gaslight, or candlelight, he sees a sparkling quick succession of yellow to green and green to yellow flashings, both beautiful and exciting to behold. Vaseline glass under modern incandescent or fluorescent light is a dull and boring yellow akin to yesterday's mashed potatoes under the glare of a refrigerator light.

The decline in popularity of Vaseline glass, starting in the last decade of the 19th century and running through the 20th century, assumed the proportions of a toboggan slide. Vaseline glass was a victim of the ordinary light bulb!

14. ATTEMPTS AT REVIVAL 1900-1941

The first 40 years of the 20th century saw attempts at revival of Vaseline glass's popularity by reintroduction of the color in its original form or by experimentation with new forms and surfaces. From a long-range merchandising point of view, all these attempts ended in failure. As stated in Chapter 7, this phenomenon was confirmed by Frank Fenton of the Fenton Art Glass Company who recalled that repeat runs of any given Vaseline glass pattern resulted in limited sales.

OPALESCENT GLASS AGAIN

The early to mid-1900s saw glass companies such as Cambridge, Fenton, Duncan and Miller, Northwood, and Tiffin periodically come out with a few elaborate pieces, such as vases, epergnes, or console sets made up of candlesticks and bowls in combination. To tap into the rising middle class market, there was also a movement toward "safe," previously successful opalescent patterns such as Spanish Lace and Daisy and Fern reissuances. Even the much-used Daisy and Button pattern from the old pattern glass heydays was trotted out and made opalescent. None of the Vaseline opalescent reissues sold well after the initial sales splurge, and their production had to be cut back or stopped.

VASELINE CARNIVAL GLASS

The late 19th century was a period of experimentation in glassmaking. Glass sales had suffered in the mass marketplace, although at the other end of the spectrum, a very expensive Tiffany art glass introduced in 1893, called "Favrile," found acceptance in the luxury glass market. What Favrile offered to the public was a new iridescent look which brought a rainbow of colors to a single-colored glass.

Fenton, Northwood, Imperial, and a few other companies saw this as an opportunity to bring the Favrile look to low-priced pressed glassware for a larger sales market. Playing it safe, they used existing glass colors, including Vaseline, and sprayed these pieces while hot with metallic salts to achieve iridescence.

Companies used different names for this glass, such as "Venetian Art," "Golden Iris," and "Radium," but the most common manufacturers' term was simply "iridescent glass." Early collectors, such as Ruth Webb Lee, called this glass "Taffeta." For decades, however, collectors have called these wares Carnival Glass, a name deriving from its use as carnival prizes.

A great deal of clear glass was sprayed with metallic salts to produce the marigold color. Glass in the base colors of blue and green was also iridized in large quantities. In comparison, relatively little Carnival glass was made by iridizing the yellow-green Vaseline color. Although these cheaply priced items enjoyed great popularity from about 1907-1915, this fad did little to revive interest in Vaseline glass.

VASELINE STRETCH GLASS

The glass companies that manufactured iridescent glass, such as Fenton, Northwood, Imperial, and Dugan, also made some glass with a stretch or onionskin effect. This was the result of finishing or shaping a piece after it was sprayed. This treatment produced a decidedly unique kind of iridescent glass. Northwood made it from 1917 to about 1922, Imperial from 1916 to the early 1920s. Fenton produced the most by far—from about 1920 to 1927.

Fenton called its uranium-based glass "Topaz" as did Northwood. Imperial called it 'lemon-yellow." Companies often produced similar wares, and it is therefore very difficult for the collector to pinpoint who made what.

Stretch glass, unlike Carnival, usually has no pattern. The decorative effect comes from the onion-skin appearance on the glass surface. Although little Carnival was made with uranium-based glass, a great deal of Topaz stretch glass was sold in the 1920s. In the short run, it prolonged the popularity of yellow-green glass, and this variation on Vaseline glass is fairly easy to find today.

OTHER REVIVAL ATTEMPTS

Heisey Glass Company tried to downplay the "old-fashioned" yellow which seemed to incite sales resistance by producing a very pale Vaseline which they called canary. They made console sets in their Narrow, Flute, Yeoman and Recessed Panel patterns. The color was a failure and Heisey discontinued it after a few years.

Fostoria took the opposite tack and turned out a darker, more amber, Vaseline with the same predictable results, even though some of their pieces were quite innovative in shape and form.

Cambridge experimented with different surface finishes such as acid-etched and copper-wheel engraving, as well as satin finishing on their "Topaz" introduced in 1922 and dropped in 1925.

GREEN VASELINE

So desperate were the glassmakers of the twenties and thirties to purge their lines of Vaseline color that they added iron to their uranium oxide dyes to put a green pastel into their glass for a more "modern" look. These pieces will fluoresce under ultraviolet light, but are definitely green with no trace of yellow. Some Vaseline collectors may collect them, but the author looks upon these aberrations as the forerunners and contemporaries of Depression glass, rather than a continuation of Vaseline glass.

The glass manufacturers got the message—only "modern colors" were acceptable, and although "Art Moderne," or, as we now call it, "Art Deco," dictated a return to glass tableware, there apparently was no room in the marketplace for Vaseline.

15. DEPRESSION AND ART DECO

Beginning in the late 1920s, a new acceptance of glass tableware appeared on the part of the public. While most of the new mass-production glass companies avoided the Vaseline color like the plague, a very few, such as the Imperial Glass Company, pressed a pattern called Beaded Block in Vaseline, U.S. Glass issued an etched pattern in Vaseline descriptively called Flower Garden with Butterfly.

These patterns in Vaseline glass hardly made it into the 1930s when they were discontinued. Although the pieces were part of the Depression glass surge, the real sales stars in Depression glass were clear "crystal," blue, green, pink, and a yellowish amber. One role of these colors was to hide the discoloration of the cheap and mass-produced glass which was often given away as premiums. The best and clearest batches were left as "crystal."

Vaseline glass, however, was never really a part of the massive Depression glass period of the thirties. Rather, Vaseline glass was made in very limited quantities for very limited and sometimes strange uses.

All through the Art Deco period of Depression glass colors and pastels, there was a small amount of Vaseline glass used in the manufacture of fancy Art Deco sculptured lamps and vases, such as those made by Phoenix and Consolidated. Few people had enough money in those days to buy such luxuries. The result was that the amount of these items made and sold was small and away from the mainstream.

For some strange reason, Vaseline glass was also used and favored for fish bowls in this period. This tradition seems to have started in the 19th century when Vaseline was in vogue. Amazingly, this usage of Vaseline for fish bowls remained unaffected by the swing away from Vaseline with practically everything else. Other exceptions were the Teaberry Gum Stand, as well as some advertising candy display jars. These pieces were for commercial purposes rather than home use.

Among the other strange items made of Vaseline glass during this period were bud vases which were held by nickel-plated fasteners and inserted on the rear interior side panels of luxury automobiles. This limited use of Vaseline glass started in the late twenties and continued through the thirties. My guess is that even though this color was unpopular during this period, it lent a sense of tradition and exclusivity appreciated by the "carriage trade."

Finally, there were the beginnings of a small collector's market, and a few astute glass manufacturers such as Fenton and Imperial would trot out the old Daisy and Button molds and press a few thousand vases, slippers, hats, toothpicks, and match holders in the old colors, including Vaseline, for sales to specialty and souvenir shops.

It was these runs of reproductions in the thirties that raised the ire of Ruth Webb Lee, who wrote in her book *Antique Fakes and Reproductions* that these so-called fakes were ruining everything for collectors of Victorian glass. Ironically, today these reproductions are as collectible as their Victorian predecessors.

It was also these reproductions that gave rise to the fiction that Vaseline glass has a "greasy" appearance and texture. The use of worn molds in conjunction with high-pressure, mass-production presses produced smooth and highly polished pieces, which together with the name "Vaseline" conjure up the idea of a greasy finish. Unfortunately, there are too many dealers and collectors who do not want to be confused by the facts and who will continue to believe that Vaseline glass is greasy.

16. Disappearance and Reappearance

Shortly after Pearl Harbor and the entrance of the United States into World War II, all uranium and its compounds were declared strategic materials, and their access to civilian uses and channels were frozen. The government was given complete control over all uranium distribution, a control which persists to this day. So little uranium was used in the glass industry at the time of the ban that its absence was hardly missed.

Between 1942 and 1952 there was almost no Vaseline glass made in the United States or anywhere else for that matter. According to Frank Fenton, the only exception would result from the use of uranium oxide already in company storage when the ban went into effect.

In 1951 there was a series of decisions by the Atomic Energy Commission relaxing the flow of uranium compounds for civilian use. These new regulations allowed for licensing of civilian firms in the purchase of uranium oxide. Various regulations were enforced on the storage and handling of this material. These regulations were later expanded to include monitoring of alpha, beta, gamma, and radon emissions.

As if the bad track record for the decade before the ban wasn't enough to dissuade glass companies from pressing Vaseline glass again, now there were also cumbersome and expensive rules and regulations to abide by. In addition, the price of uranium oxide was over $8.50 per pound. It is no wonder, therefore, that most glass companies decided to ignore Vaseline glass completely, and only few companies made it at all in the 1950s.

Tentatively and only in small quantities, a few Daisy and Button pieces began to appear, followed by some opalescent items. The intended market was a small but growing number of collectors.

In the 1960s and '70s additional small glass companies, such as Mosser, Degenhart, Boyd, and Summit Art Glass, began catering to this new collector's market. All these companies featured Vaseline as a color and made items in the hundreds rather than in the thousands or hundreds of thousands as their predecessors did. In most cases, the items pressed were relatively small, and even tiny, in order to get the most pieces out of each batch. One company even made pressings of one-inch butter pats in Vaseline!

Fenton made some opalescent Vaseline glass pieces during this period, turning out beautiful items in their Cactus pattern. Pairpoint Glass Company, made some console sets in their "Canaria" Vaseline color with their exclusive "Captive Bubble Connector."

Even New York's Metropolitan Museum of Art had the Imperial Glass Company press a few hundred Dolphin candlesticks, flip glasses and early bottles in Vaseline from molds made from the old pieces themselves, but with pressed initials "MMA" on the bases of all the pieces. In some cases, unscrupulous individuals have ground the initials from these pieces and sold them for exorbitant prices as "Sandwich Glass" to a gullible public.

From the 1960s until about 1982, the Westmoreland Glass Company made a small amount of Vaseline glass each year. Westmoreland had acquired a number of old molds from defunct glass companies in order to make reissues for the collectors' market. When Westmoreland went out of business in 1984, its molds and other assets were sold.

Soon companies like Summit and Viking were pressing children's water and punch bowl sets in Vaseline a few hundred pieces at a time, items which Westmoreland had only pressed in clear or milk glass. There were also Vaseline pressings of earlier pieces, such as the Cambridge Lady and the Atterbury Rabbit, which had never been pressed in Vaseline before. The key to these pressings is that they were of small quantity and not repeated.

Also pressed recently in Vaseline were various measuring cups, reamers, and shot glasses of the Depression Era which also had never before been pressed in Vaseline. Again, the collector should know that these pieces have been pressed only in small quantities. Because of restrictions, only limited amounts of uranium oxide could be purchased and stored by each company.

Since the first edition of this book was written, interviews with three men involved in the manufacture of Vaseline glass have shed new light on this matter. Their perspectives show differences between greater and lesser use of uranium oxide in glassmaking.

Frank Fenton headed the Fenton Art Glass Company from 1948 until his retirement in the mid-1980s. The Fenton company used a large amount of uranium oxide to make Custard, Burmese, Topaz opalescent, and Vaseline glass. At one point, the government limited Fenton to 250 lbs. of uranium oxide. The supplier, however, would only ship this chemical in 500 lb. drums! Mr. Fenton recalls that it took nearly a year to get this conflict resolved. As a fairly large consumer, Fenton Art Glass was very conscious of strict government regulations.

Dwight Johnson was chemist for the Westmoreland Glass Company from the early 1960s to 1982. Here are his recollections: "Each year we acquired about 25 lbs. of depleted uranium oxide from McKesson Robbins, a Pittsburgh chemical company. They helped us get the necessary government permit and told us how much we could buy, based on availability. I used 3 lbs. of uranium oxide in a pot holding 1000 lbs. of glass, so I made about eight pots a year. Altogether I mixed more than 100 batches of Vaseline glass.

"There weren't many restrictions in using this black powdery stuff. I was required to keep it in a locked storeroom, and I had the only key. I had to wear rubber gloves and goggles while mixing a batch. Since I'll be 80 years old in a few days, I don't think it did me any lasting harm!

"I used cadmium sulphide to make a bright yellow glass and flowers of sulphur to make a brown-tinted yellow. The yellow-green Vaseline color is unique, and I don't think it can be made without uranium oxide."

Government restrictions may have eased over the years, making it more feasible for small glassmaking operations to manufacture a limited amount of Vaseline glass. John Boyd of Boyd's Crystal Art Glass explains that two rules govern his company's use of uranium oxide for making Vaseline glass: first, no more than 15 pounds can be stored at one time; secondly, the batch cannot contain more than 1% of the uranium oxide. In contrast, Boyd says that the Primrose color made years ago by the Cambridge Glass Company contained fully 3% uranium oxide.

17. The Future

What does the future hold for Vaseline glass and its collectors? One doesn't need a crystal ball to foresee that anything fragile and breakable made in limited quantities will be scarce in the future.

It is safe to contend that the environmental and safety considerations which prompted the rules and regulations governing the production of Vaseline glass will not be relaxed. Neither is it likely that the cost of uranium compounds will decrease. Rather, it more likely that these factors will move in the opposite direction, keeping future Vaseline glass production on a very limited basis.

Scarcity has a way of making people forget about what is "new" and what is "old," and what is a "reproduction." All Vaseline glass is collectible as long as it is genuine, and, since there is an easy test of verification, the value restrictions of age, origin, and reissuance do not apply to this glass as they do to other collectibles. By far the greatest barometer of value is scarcity rather than age. The examples of gold and diamonds point out this fact.

Values of these wares should rise in the future even though some Vaseline glass will still be made, albeit on a limited level. The analogy which applies is that of increased values for gold and diamonds even though they are still being mined. Also, like gold and diamonds, Vaseline glass is verifiable. A simple black light test will determine authentic Vaseline glass from its imitators. No such test exists for most other categories of collectibles.

All speculative and financial considerations aside, Vaseline glass, with its hauntingly beautiful yellow-green reflections and breathtaking fluorescent glows, will retain its magic and mystery for generations yet to come.

NOTES ON THE ORIGINAL COLOR PLATES

The following 32 pages of color plates reflect the beauty, variety and diversity of the magic glass, Yellow-Green Vaseline! The articles shown here are from many different factories and eras in the history of glassmaking.

Items are individually numbered throughout the color plates, and captions keyed to these numbers may be found immediately after the expanded color section.

After you've perused the first 30 color plates, you may be ready to take the quiz on page 79!

1

2

3

4

5

6

7

8

9

10

11

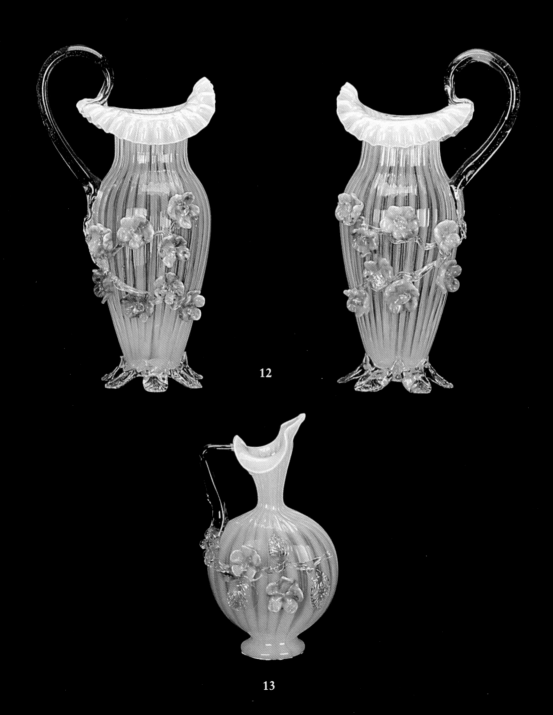

12

13

14

15

16

17

18

19

20

21

22

23

24

25

26

27

28

29

30

31

32

33

34

35

36

37

38   39   40   41

42 43 44 45 46 47

48 49 50 51 52

53

54

55

56

57

58

59

60

61

62

63

64

65

66

67

68

69

70

71

72

73

74

75

76

77

78

79

80

81

82

83

84

85   86   87   88   89   90   91

92   93   94

95   96   97   98   99

100   101   102   103   104   105   106

107

108

109

110

111

112

113

57

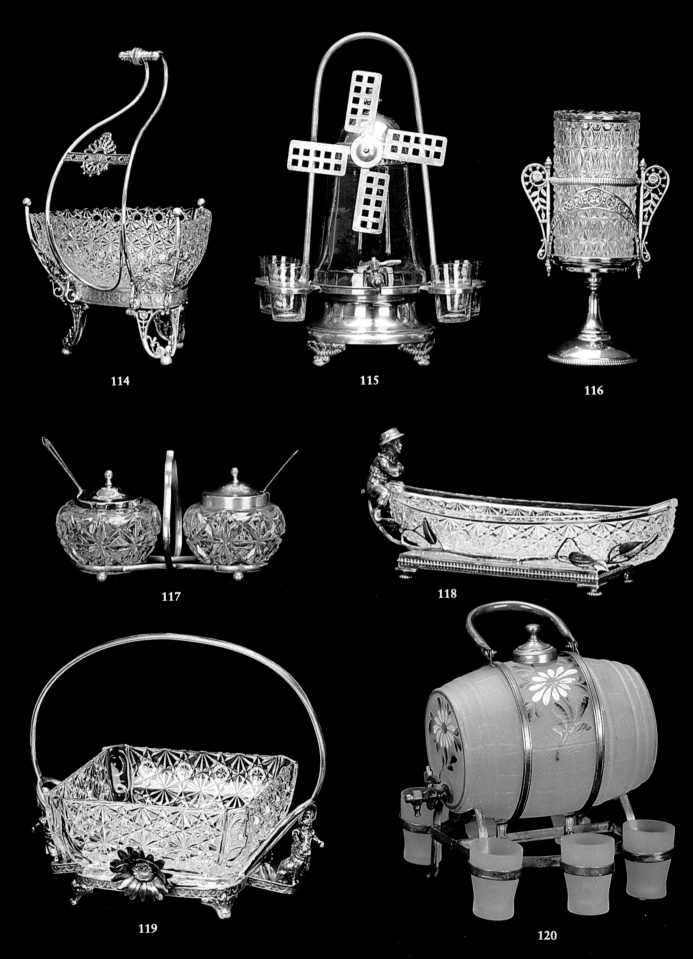

114

115

116

117

118

119

120

122

123

122

121

125

126

124

127

128

129

130

131

132

133

134

135

136

137

59

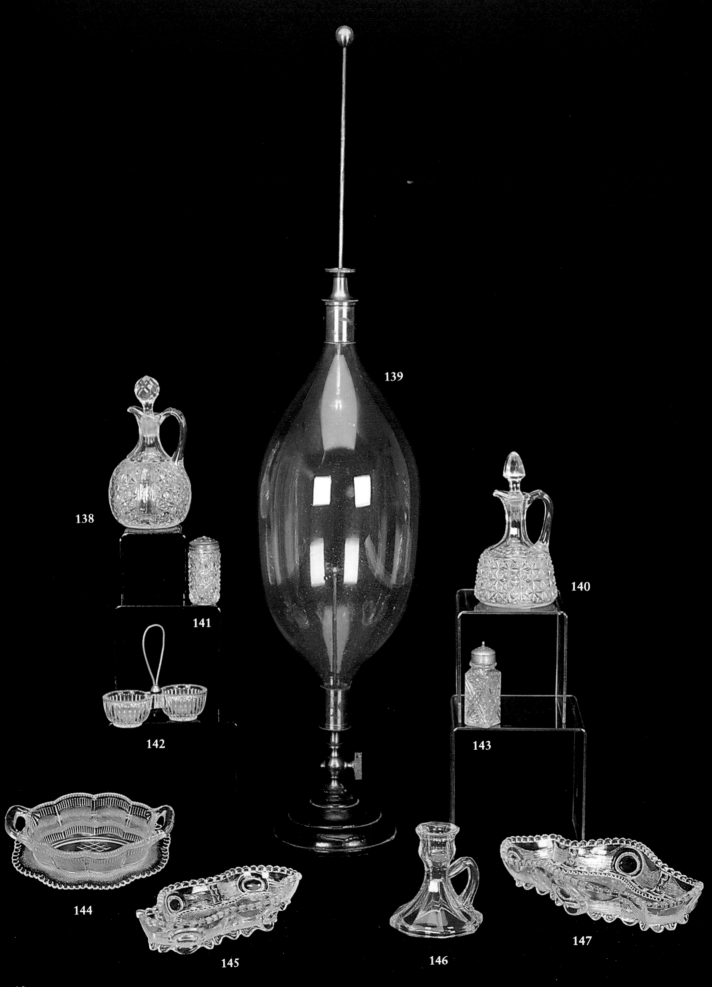

138

139

140

141

142

143

144

145

146

147

148   149   150   151   152   153

154   155   156   157   158   159   160

161   162   163   164

165   166   167   168   169   170   171

172

173

174

175

176

177

178

179

180

181

182

183

184

185

186

187

188

189

190

191

190

192

193

194

195

196

197

198

199

200

201

202

203

204

205

206

207

208

209

210

211

212

213

214

215

216

217

218

219

220

221

222

223

224

64

225

226

227

228

229

230

231

232

233

234

235

236

237

238

239

240

241

65

242

243

244

245

246

247

248

249

250

251

252

253

254

255

256

257

258

259

260

261

262

263

264

265

266

267

268

269

270

271

272

273

274

275

276

277

278

279

280A

280B

281

282

283

284

285

286 287 288

289 290 291 292

293 294 295

296 297

69

298

299

300

301

302

303

304

305

306

307

308

309

310

311

311

311

312

313

314

315

316

317

318

319

320

320

320

321

322

323

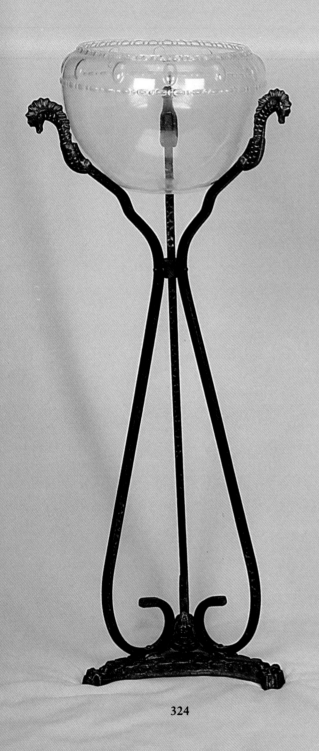

324

325

326   327   328   329   330   331   332

333   334   335   336   337

338   339   340   341

342 343 344 345 346

347 348 349

351 352 353 350

354 355 356 357 358 359 360 361

362 363 364 365 366 367

368

369

370

371

372

373

374

375

376

377

378

379

380

381

382

383

384

385

386

387

388

389

390

391

392

393

394

395

396

397

398

399

400

401

402

403

404

405

406

407

408

409

410

411

412

413

414

415

416

417

418

419

420

421

422

423

424

425

426

427

428

429

430

431

432

433

434

435

436

437

438 439 440 441

442 443 444 445

Which of these **isn't** genuine Vaseline glass?   Turn the page!

446   447   448   449   450   451 452

453   454   455   456   457

Now you know! The little creamer **is not** genuine Vaseline glass!

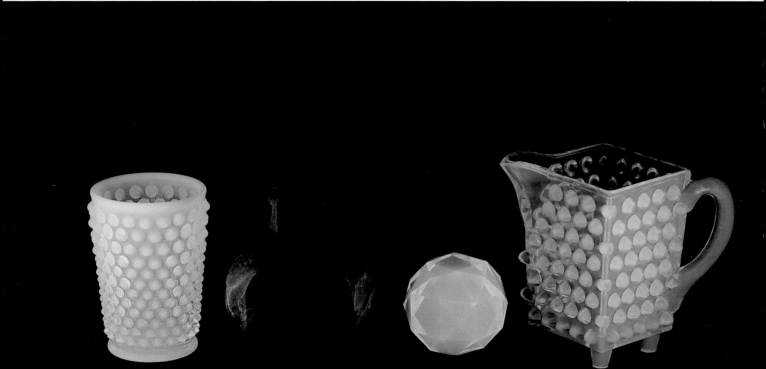

NOTES ON SUPPLEMENTARY COLOR PAGES

This section adds nearly
150 items to the pieces shown
in color in the first edition.

These examples of Vaseline glass are
varied—some are true antiques while others
are recent collectibles. Many are decorated
with some kind of surface treatment —
acid etching, cutting, or enameling.

These diverse shapes have one thing in common.
Since all have uranium oxide as a coloring ingredient, they
belong to the family of wares that we call "the magic glass."

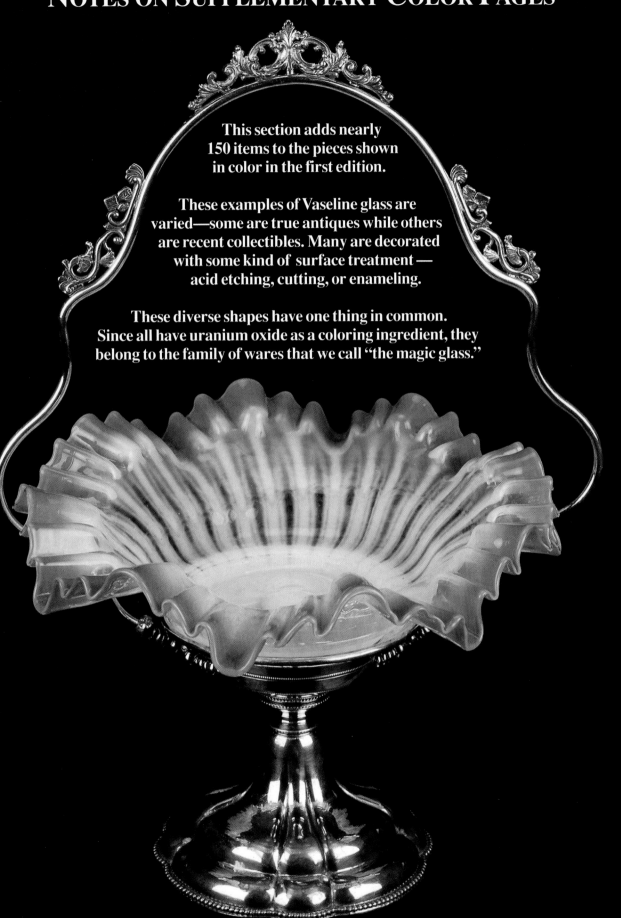

458

459

460

461

462

463

464

465

466

467

468

469

470

471

472

473

474

475

476

477

478

479

480

481

482

483

484

485

486

487

488

489

490

491

492

493

494

495

496

497

498

85

499   500   501

502   503   504

505   506

507   508   509

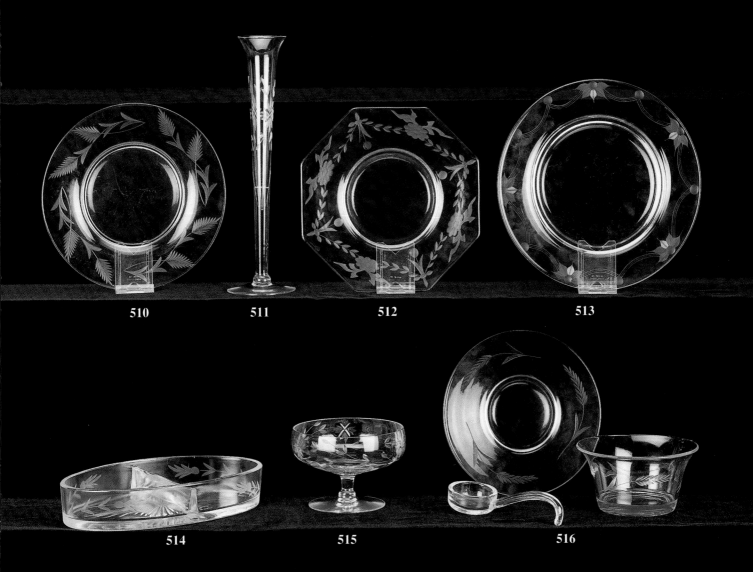

510   511   512   513

514   515   516

517

519

520   521   522

523   524   525   526

527   528   529

530

531

532

533

534

535

536

537

538 539 540 541 542 543

544 545 546 547

89

548 549 550 551 552

553 554 555 556

557 558

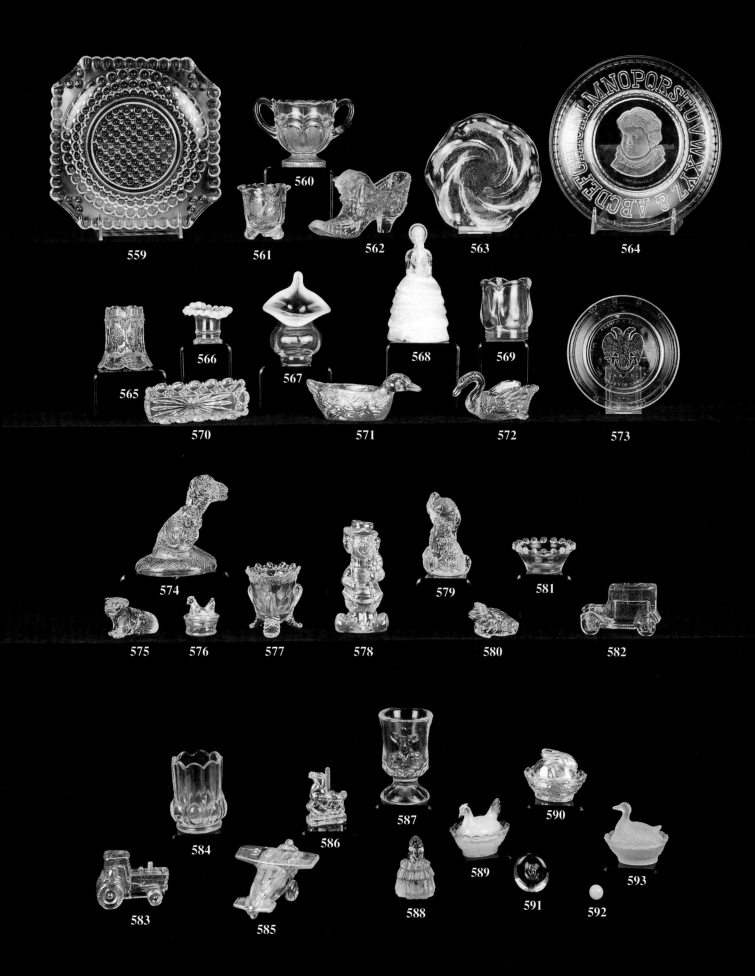

559   560   561   562   563   564

565   566   567   568   569   570   571   572   573

574   575   576   577   578   579   580   581   582

583   584   585   586   587   588   589   590   591   592   593

Significant Vaseline Pieces Not Illustrated

A (1) Dolphin candlesticks (pr) 10¾ inches tall with square base. Sandwich or New England Glass Co. ca. 1870's.

   (2) Same as above but with MMA (Metropolitan Museum of Art) mold mark. ca. 1970's.

B   Whale oil lamp. Sandwich or New England Glass Co. or McKee. ca. 1860's.

C   Log Cabin covered compote on stand. Central Glass Co. ca. 1870's.

D   Wheelbarrow with pewter wheel 9½" long x 5½" w. x 3" t. Button and Daisy. Gillinder. Souvenir at 1876 Centennial in Philadelphia.

E   Covered sugar Flower Pot. Adams Glass Co. ca. 1870's.

F   Hand painted Bohemian decanter. Mold blown ca. 1860's.

G   Figural fish covered dish 7" long x 5" w. x 2¾" t. ca. 1880's.

H   Figural bird with berry in beak, covered mustard. Flint. Acorn finial. McKee. ca. 1880's.

I   "Balky Mule" tray (Currier & Ives) Bellaire Goblet Co. ca. 1886.

J   Sleigh salt 6" long x 4" w. x 3" t. Campbell, Jones-without patent date. U.S. Glass—with 1886 date (Produced by U.S. Glass in 1899-1901).

K   "Radium Vitalizer" quack cure liquid dispenser 18" t. ca. 1900.

L   Military hat toothpick/match holder. U.S. Glass Co. ca. 1902.

M   Slipper match holder. Button & Daisy. 6⅛" long x 2" h. Central Glass Co. ca. 1882.

N   Pump and Trough. Opalescent. Northwood (some pumps signed in script) ca. 1899.

O   Dolphin compote. Opalescent. Northwood ca. 1899.

P   Tree Trunk vase. Opalescent. Northwood ca. 1905.

Q   Jewel box. Hand painted flowers with black glass lid. 5" sq. x 4" t. Silver plated stand ca. 1910.

R   Opalescent globe light fixture. Geometric designs in Art Deco stepped pattern, 24" w. x 18" t. ca. 1936.

S   Fluted strawholder. Nickle top 10½"t. ca. 1937.

T   Art Deco bowl held by kneeling, chrome plated nude. Frankart. ca. 1936.

U   Cat figural bottle 8" t. Fenton. ca. 1950's.

Sugar-Water Set. An outstanding and unique presentation set of early (ca. 1839-41) Bohemian cut uranium glass. Harrach Glassworks, possibly a gift from the Count of Harrach.

JOSEPH RIEDEL (1816-1894), first to use uranium oxide in glassmaking.

Small vase of Anna Gelb (Yellow), cut and decorated with red glazing, ca. 1845.

Both the cup and this vase were made as presentation pieces and were produced only in tiny quantities due to high costs.

ANNA M. RIEDEL, eldest daughter of Joseph. The first Vaseline glass, called Anna Gelb, was named for her.

Small cup of Anna Gelb, cut and decorated with gold (dated 1841).

Three beautiful examples of late 19th century Bohemian (Czech) cut Vaseline glass. Though less expensive than the earlier pieces, still was not made in mass production.

Klondyke and Alaska

KLONDYKE.

In Crystal, Green,
Pearl Yellow and
Pearl Blue.

ALASKA.

Opalescent and Decorated
Lemonade Sets IN LARGE VARIETY AND AT RIGHT PRICES.

THE NORTHWOOD CO.,

INDIANA, PA.

NEW YORK,
Frank M. Miller,
76 Park Place.

PHILADELPHIA,
Fitzpatrick & Pascoe,
930 Arch Street.

BALTIMORE,
Andrew J. George.

WEST, Carl Northwood.   **EAST, George Mortimer.**

Northwood Glass Co., ca. 1898.

YOU HAVE SEEN THE

KLONDYKE.

⇒ THIS IS THE ⇐

ALASKA.

THE NORTHWOOD CO., Indiana, Pa.

Northwood Glass Co., ca. 1898.

THE KLONDYKE

Made in Pearl Flint, Pearl Blue, Pearl Gold and Fine Crystal.

Pressed Sugar and Cover.

The Northwood Co., Indiana, Pa.

New York, A. G. Menzies, 46 West Broadway.   Philadelphia, Fitzpatrick & Pascoe, 930 Arch St.   Boston, Chase & Francis, 122 Pearl St.
Baltimore, J. Beiswanger, Jr. & Co., Baltimore and Hanover Sts.   West, Carl Northwood.   East, George Mortimer.

Northwood Glass Co., ca. 1898.

Northwood Glass Co., ca. 1898.

Austrian pattern, Indiana Tumbler and Goblet Co., ca. 1897.

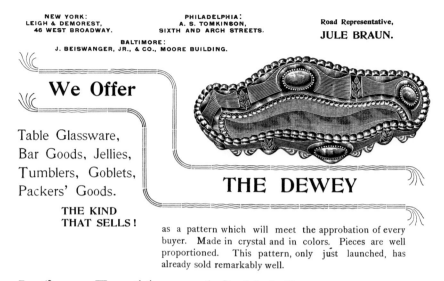

Dewey pattern, Indiana Tumbler and Goblet Co., ca. 1898.

Dewey pattern, Indiana Tumbler and Goblet Co., ca. 1898.

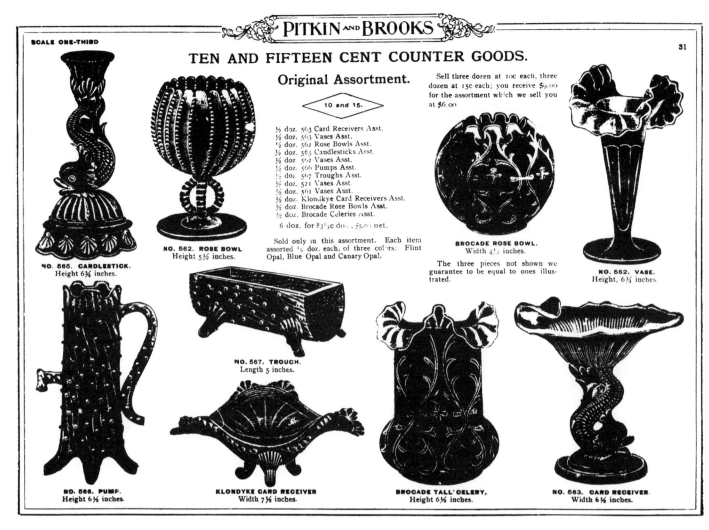

TEN AND FIFTEEN CENT COUNTER GOODS.

Original Assortment.

◇ 10 and 15. ◇

½ doz. 563 Card Receivers Asst.
½ doz. 563 Vases Asst.
½ doz. 562 Rose Bowls Asst.
½ doz. 565 Candlesticks Asst.
½ doz. 562 Vases Asst.
½ doz. 566 Pumps Asst.
½ doz. 567 Troughs Asst.
½ doz. 521 Vases Asst.
½ doz. 561 Vases Asst.
½ doz. Klondkye Card Receivers Asst.
½ doz. Brocade Rose Bowls Asst.
½ doz. Brocade Celeries Asst.

6 doz. for 83⅓c doz., $5.00 net.

Sold only in this assortment. Each item assorted ⅙ doz. each, of three colors: Flint Opal, Blue Opal and Canary Opal.

Sell three dozen at 10c each, three dozen at 15c each; you receive $9.00 for the assortment which we sell you at $6.00

The three pieces not shown we guarantee to be equal to ones illustrated.

NO. 565. CANDLESTICK.
Height 6¾ inches.

NO. 562. ROSE BOWL
Height 5½ inches.

BROCADE ROSE BOWL.
Width 4½ inches.

NO. 562. VASE.
Height, 6¾ inches.

NO. 567. TROUGH.
Length 5 inches.

NO. 566. PUMP.
Height 6¼ inches.

KLONDYKE CARD RECEIVER
Width 7½ inches.

BROCADE TALL CELERY.
Height 6½ inches.

NO. 563. CARD RECEIVER.
Width 6½ inches.

SCALE ONE-THIRD

Assortment of opalescent novelties, Northwood Glass Co., ca. 1899.

No. 173. Pickle Castor. Assorted Colors. (Height 12 inches.)
$5.50.

Pickle castor with Vaseline glass insert, ca. 1890.

Opaline Brocade pattern (now called Spanish Lace), Northwood Glass Co., ca. 1899.

Pickle castor with Vaseline glass insert, ca. 1890

Iris pattern (now called Iris with Meander), Jefferson Glass Co., ca. 1903.

National/Dugan's Inverted Fan and Feather rose bowl, ca. 1901.

Northwood's Beads and Bark vase, ca. 1904.

Northwood's Town Pump, ca. 1899.

Fish-in-the-Sea vase, manufacturer unknown.

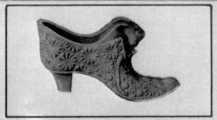

Two catalog reprints, ca. 1937. Reprinted from *Fenton Glass: The Second Twenty-Five Years.*

FEBRUARY SPECIAL

CRYSTAL, ROSE, VASELINE, AQUAMARINE

DAISY & BUTTON PATTERN

1900 SALAD SET

1—10″ Bowl.   1—13″ Plate.

*WRITE FOR SPECIAL PRICE
TO STIMULATE RETAIL SALES.*

FENTON ART GLASS CO.
WILLIAMSTOWN, W. VA.

THE L. G. WRIGHT COMPANY

MANUFACTURERS

OF

PRESSED AND BLOWN GLASSWARE

NEW MARTINSVILLE, W. VA.

September 1, 1938

Mrs. L.P. Fletcher
Painted Post, N.Y. R #1

Dear Madam:

Received an order from you for several pieces of merchandise about which we thought it best to write you, listing the items, colors, and prices and in that way we will not make any mistakes in shipping you merchandise.

We would like for you to look this list over and make up a new order and send it to us.

Westward Ho Goblets	$ 9.00 doz
" " Sauces	9.00 doz
Daisy and Button Goblets Asst. Colors	7.20 doz
" " " Sq. Plates Blue,Vaseline, Amber, Crystal	6.00 doz
Moon and Star Goblets	9.00 doz
Pineapple "	9.00 doz
Rose and Snow " Asst. Colors	7.20 doz
Baltimore Pear "	12.00 doz
" " Plates	1.25 ea.
Three Face Sauce Dishes	2.00 ea.
Rose and Snow Plates Asst. Colors	1.00 ea.
Barber Bottles Amber, Vaseline	5.00 pr.
" " Cranberry Red,Opalescent Blue	4.00 ea.
Hobnail Cream Pitchers Cranberry Red and Opalescent Blue	4.00 ea.
" Cruits Cranberry Red and Opalescent Blue	4.00 ea.
Candy Stripe Swirl Water Pitchers	3.00 ea.
Blue Opalescent Sq. Mouth Dotted Water Pitcher	3.00 ea.
Duck Salts, Milk, Green	3.00 doz.

Will have several new items by the 20th of Sept.

We wish that you would make your order from the above list and send it to us at once.

Very truly yours,

LW:VW   L.G. Wright Co.

NO. 7 CHERRY PATTERN

CHERRY PATTERN

1963

A-Amber	AM-Amethyst	R-Ruby
B-Blue	AR-Amberina	S-Slag
G-Green	VA-Vaseline	

Item No.		Price Each
7-1	Bowl Footed Large Shallow, Regular A. B. G. AM. AR.	$ 4.75 / 5.75
7-2	Butter and Cover A. G. AR.	2.00 / 2.50
7-3	Compote 6" Open Scroll A. G. S.	1.25 / 1.50
7-4	Cream Pitcher A. B. G. VA. AR. R. S.	1.25 / 1.50
7-5	Sugar Vase A. B. G. VA. AR. R. S.	1.25 / 1.50
7-6	Salt Dip A. B. G. AM. AR.	.75 / .95
7-7	Salver Large Ftd. A. B. G. AM. AR.	4.75 / 5.75
7-8	Toothpick A. B. G. AM. AR. R.	.55 / .70
7-9	Tumbler A. B.	1.05
7-10	Water Pitcher A. B.	3.75

7-4 CHERRY PATTERN CREAM
Amber, Blue, Green, Vaseline, Amberina, Ruby, Slag

7-4

7-5 CHERRY PATTERN SUGAR
Amber, Blue, Green, Vaseline, Amberina, Ruby, Slag

7-5

7-10 CHERRY WATER PITCHER
Amber, Blue

7-10

7-1 CHERRY LARGE FOOTED BOWL REGULAR ALSO SHALLOW
Amber, Blue, Green, Amethyst, Amberina

7-1

THE L. G. WRIGHT COMPANY

MANUFACTURERS

OF

PRESSED AND BLOWN GLASSWARE

NEW MARTINSVILLE, W. VA.

" 1938 Inventory "

7	dozen - #2 Basket	@ --	$ 3.00	- $	21.00
6	" -- #3 "	@	4.20		25.20
48	" ----- D. and B. Goblets	@	1.50		72.00
28	" ----- " " " Plates, round	@	3.50		98.00
29	" ----- " " " square	@	1.35		39.15
35	" ----- Rose and Snow "	@	1.35		47.25
42	" ----- " " " " Goblets	@	1.50		61.00
6	" ----- Westward Ho "	@	2.25		13.50
4	" ----- " " Sauces	@	2.75		11.00
5	" ----- Moon and Star Goblets	@	1.50		7.50
1	" ----- " " " Bowl	@	6.00		6.00
6	" ----- D. and B. Pannel Goblet				
	Blue, Amber	@	3.50		21.00
14	" ----- Horn of Plenty Tumbler	@	2.00		28.00
18	" ----- Pear Goblets	@	1.50		27.00
1-1/2	" ----- Grape "	@	1.50		2.25
7	" ----- Thumbprint Goblets, R.S.	@	3.94		13.58
12	" ----- " " Crystal	@	1.02		12.24
1	" ----- Hand Vase	@	4.50		4.50
5	" ----- Fan Trays	@	3.00		15.00
7	" ----- Kitten Slippers	@	1.80		12.60
1	" ----- Spot Pitchers	@	12.00		12.00
20	only ----- Turkeys	@	1.00		20.00
26	" ----- Barber Bottles, Cranberry	@	1.50		39.00
14	" ----- " " Blue	@	1.00		14.00
30	" ----- " " Am. Vas.	@	1.00		30.00
60	" ----- Hobnail Pitcher, Cranberry	@	1.50		90.00
30	" ----- " " Blue	@	1.00		30.00
20	" ----- " Cruits "	@	1.00		20.00
18	" ----- " Vases "	@	.75		13.50
12	dozen ----- Lion Goblets,Cry. Frosted	@	2.75		33.00
3	" ----- " Plates	@	4.50		13.50
6	" ----- Three Face Goblet	@	2.75		16.50
15	" ----- " " Wine	@	2.75		41.25
4	" ----- " " Sauce	@	3.00		12.00
1	" ----- Pear Plates	@	3.00		3.00
4	dozen - #1 Chicken, White	@ --	$ 3.00	- $	12.00
2	" -- #2 " Black	@	6.00		12.00
10	" -- #1 Duck White	@	1.50		15.00
2	" -- #1 Camels "	@	4.20		8.40
5	" ----- Kitten Plates & Rabbit	@	3.00		15.00
1	" ----- Zodiac " Large	@	6.00		6.00
2	" ----- " " Small	@	3.00		6.00
4	" ----- Turtles	@	4.32		17.28
3	" ----- Elephants	@	2.70		8.10
3	" ----- Bears	@	3.24		9.72
2	" ----- Frogs	@	2.70		5.40
190	" -- #1 Slipper	@	.60		114.00
79	" -- #2 "	@	.76		60.04
138	" -- #1 Hat	@	1.00		138.00
33	" -- #2 "	@	2.00		66.00
12	" -- #3 "	@	3.00		36.00

Total Stock on Hand $ 1451.46

ILLUSTRATED VASELINE PIECES

Abbreviations: F.A.G.C.A. - Fenton Art Glass Collectors of America
(FMF) - Frank M. Fenton   **(Yalom) -** Libby Yalom

1 - Pair of 8^1/$_2$" candlesticks. No longer believed to be Sandwich or McKee. Probably English.

2 - Bon bon dish. Mold blown, hand crimped 6" tall hand applied to ball connector base, New England Glass. Mid-19th Century. Flint.

3 - 8" tall covered syrup with underplate. Probably made by Cambridge in the 1920s. See *Colors in Cambridge Glass*, 1984; National Cambridge Collectors, plate 10.

4 - 5" tall flint bonbon dish. Possibly McKee, ca. 1860s.

5 - Flint 3^1/$_2$" tall perfume, ca. 1860s.

6 - Drapery tie backs, 4^1/$_2$" diameter, pewter rods. Flint. Sandwich.

7 - Master salt 2" x 3^1/$_2$", Flint, ca. 1860s.

8 - "Christmas" Salt and Pepper Shakers. Patent date Dec. 25, 1877. Shaker has agitator. Possibly the only pieces accurately attributed to Boston and Sandwich Glass Co.

9 - Lady's mucilage pot. Cut flint dated "7th DEC'R 1840." Possibly Sandwich, 2^1/$_2$" tall.

10 - Whiskey taster. Flint. Sandwich or New England Glass Co., ca. 1870s.

11 - Hexagonal match holder, 3" tall Flint, ca. 1860s.

12 - Pair of 12" opalescent glass ewers. Hand applied flowers and handles. Hobbs, Brockunier, ca. 1870s.

13 - Opalescent glass bulbous ewer. Applied amber handle, applied flowers. Hobbs, Brockunier, ca. 1870s.

14 - Celery vase. Column Block (Panel and Star), O'Hara Glass, ca. 1880.

15 - This shallow bowl is Clio, not Daisy and Button (per original caption). Challinor, Taylor, & Co., ca.1891, Factory C of U.S. Glass. Daisy & Button does not have a pattern in the button. See *U.S. Glass from A-Z*; Heacock and Bickenheuser; 1978; Antique Publications, pg. 89.

16 - Tobacco or cigar humidor. Honeycomb. Maker unknown, ca. 1886.

17 - Silver top for above. Victorian girl's face.

18 - Sugar bowl. Oaken Bucket. Bryce Bros., ca. 1880s.

19 - Creamer. Oaken Bucket. Bryce Bros., ca. 1880s.

20 - Sugar bowl. Three Panel. Richards & Hartley, ca. 1880.

21 - Creamer. Three Panel. Richards & Hartley, ca. 1880.

22 - 6^1/$_2$" tall sugar bowl. Lattice & Thumbprint (#796) by Central Glass, 1880s. Also known as Rope & Thumbprint. See *Pattern Glass Preview* #4; Heacock, pg. 7.

23 - Cruet. Dewey. Indiana Tumbler & Goblet, ca. 1898.

24 - Silver-covered jelly jar with shell spoon. Honeycomb, maker unknown, ca. 1870.

25 - Mug. Dewey. Indiana Tumbler & Goblet, ca. 1898.

26 - Syrup jar. Applied handle. Zinc top. Inverted Thumbprint.

27 - Pedestal fruit bowl. Rose Sprig. 7" tall, 10" diameter. Campbell, Jones & Co., ca. 1886.

28 - Match holder with striker and Daisy & Button sides. George Duncan and Sons, ca. 1886.

29 - Wildflower creamer. U.S. Glass, ca. 1891. Reproduced by L.G. Wright. (FMF)

30 - Maple Leaf (Diamond Center) platter, non-flint, maker unknown, ca. 1885. See *Early American Pattern Glass 1850-1910*; Jenks & Luna; 1990; Wallace-Homestead, pg. 350.

31 - Water set - pitcher, tumbler, tray. Lattice & Thumbprint (#796) by Central Glass, c. 1880s. See #22.

32 - Spooner. Medallion. U.S. Glass, ca. 1891.

33 - Covered compote. Maple Leaf. Gillinder & Sons, ca. 1888.

34 - 8" Plate Woodbury. Imperial Glass Co., ca. 1920. See *Colored Glassware of the Depression Era 2*, Hazel Marie Weatherman, pg. 160.

35 - Fish relish dish with upturned tail. Cathedral. Bryce Bros., ca. 1888.

36 - Pilgrim Syrup Bottle. Belmont Glass and Goblet, ca. 1882.

37 - Covered candy dish. A Grasshopper variation, maker unattributed, ca. 1880s. See *Kamm, #9*, 1970, pg. 57, or possibly Diamond & Sunburst variant, non-flint, Bryce Bros., ca.1882.

38 - Platter 8" x 13". Deer and Pine Tree. McKee, ca. 1880s.

39 - Two-handled Platter. Pimlico. New Martinsville, ca. 1902.

40 - Sauce Dish. Dewdrop with Star. Campbell, Jones & Co., ca. 1884.

41 - Notched platter, 8" x 12", ca. 1875.

42 - Cigarette/Match Holder, Daisy & Button. U.S. Glass Co., ca. 1892.

43 - Salters. Tree of Life. Portland Glass Co., ca. 1867. Other companies made variations.

44 - Covered compote. Pressed Diamond. Central Glass Co., ca. 1886.

45 - Toothpick holder. Thousand Eye. Richards and Hartley, ca. 1890.

46 - Cup. Hobnail. Possibly McKee, ca. 1872.

47 - Child's butter. Basketweave.

48 - Bowl 8" oval. Two Panel. Richards & Hartley, ca. 1880.

49 - Spooner in the Stork pattern introduced by A.A. Importing Co. in1982. Made from a new mold. A copy of the original, which was not made in Vaseline. See *Identifying Pattern Glass Reproductions*; Jenks, Luna & Reilly; 1993; Wallace-Homestead, pg. 278.

50 - Celery holder, 8" tall Flint. Diamond & Prism, ca. 1860. Rare.

51 - This Monkey spooner was not originally produced in Vaseline. It was introduced by A.A. Importing Co. in 1975. See *Identifying Pattern Glass Reproductions*: Jenks, Luna & Reilly; 1993; Wallace-Homestead, pg. 224.

52 - This spooner is not Medallion, it is another variation of Grasshopper. See explanation for #37.

53 - Whiskbroom figural dish, Campbell, Jones & Co., ca. 1880s. The Whisk pickle dish was also made by Geo. Duncan & Sons, ca. 1886. It has been reproduced. See *Victorian Novelties and Figurals*; Neila & Tom Bredehoft.

54 - Hand with Daisy and Button cornucopia. Geo. Duncan, ca. 1890. Latter production by U.S. Glass. Larger version made by Fenton in 1941. (FMF)

55 - Covered butter. Bell with clapper cover, ca. 1880s.

56 - Bottle figural dish, ca. 1880s.

57, 58 - Bee figural butter dish. Bryce Bros., ca. 1889.

59 - Sad Iron figural butter dish. U.S. Glass Co., ca. 1890s.

60 - Toothpick holder. Dog with Hat. Belmont Glass, ca. 1885.

61 - Cow figural butter dish. Bryce Bros., ca. 1880s.

62 - Salt & Pepper in caddy. Daisy & Button. U.S. Glass Co., ca. 1890s.

63 - The Spice barrel is Fine Cut & Block by King & Sons, ca. 1885. See *Glass Collector's Digest*, Feb/March 1995, pg. 71.

64 - The Tramp shoe from the 1890s was made only in milk glass. Degenhart made an unmarked shoe from 1962-1972. Signed shoes were made from 1972-1978. Shoes carrying the Boyd mark were made from 1978 on. See *Shoes of Glass*; Libby Yalom; plate 40, #524, explanation pg. 116; plate 49, #598, explanation pg. 122.

65 - This slipper is not the Bryce shoe, patent Oct 19/86, which has smaller daisies and is 4½" long. This slipper appears to be the salt made by Geo. Duncan & Sons, ca. 1887. It has been reproduced. See *Shoes of Glass*; Libby Yalom; plate 39, #510, explanation pg.115.

66 - This roller skate was made by the Central Glass Co., ca. 1870-1885. See *Shoes of Glass*; Libby Yalom; plate 13, #157, explanation pg. 80.

67 - The same bootee appears in *Shoes of Glass*; Libby Yalom; plate 18, #219, explanation. pg. 89. Maker unknown.

68 - 12" shoe relish or celery dish. Hobbs, Brockunier & Co., ca. 1884. (Yalom)

69 - Covered mustard. Art Nouveau Bird on Tree Trunk, ca. 1900.

70 - Top hat. Duncan, ca. 1890s. Fenton also made this item in 1937.

71 - High button shoe on pedestal base. Perfume Bottle Holder. (B&H on pedestal stands for Bean & Hurlbut, designers), Bellaire Goblet Co., ca. 1888.

72 - Coal scuttle with nickle-plated handle and shovel. Daisy & Button, ca. 1880s.

73 - 7" Shoe. Bryce Bros., ca. 1886.

74 - Columbia Bread Tray, 11" x 9", U.S. Glass, ca. 1890s.

75 - "Give Us This Day…" Bread Tray. Campbell, Jones & Co., ca. 1870s.

76 - Knights of Labor Bread Plate. Bakewell, Pears and Co., ca. 1879.

77 - Rural scene tray. Basketweave, ca. 1885. This has been reproduced.

78 - Grant Peace Plate, 10" diameter. Maple Leaf, Gillinder & Sons, ca. 1888.

79 - Door knobs, possible McKee, ca. 1889.

80 - Small cup. Souvenir "World's Fair" 1892. Libbey Glass Co.

81 - Cut glass faceted paperweight. Flint.

82 - Bud vase, Wheat Sheave, "World's Fair souvenir 1893". Libbey Glass Co.

83 - This piece is a piano insulator, non-flint, by McKee, ca.1915-1920s. See *Complete Book of McKee Glass*; Stout; 1972; pg. 210.

84 - Furniture caster. Non Flint, ca. 1890s.

85 - Etched 7$^{1}/_{2}$" cologne bottle, cut glass stopper, ca. 1880s.

86 - Etched 6$^{1}/_{2}$" applied handle bath oil bottle, cut glass stopper, ca. 1880s.

87 - Blown glass decanter 9", blown stopper, ca. 1890s.

88 - Fully cut decanter 5", ca. 1880s.

89 - Apothecary bottle, ca. 1890s.

90 - Blown decanter, ca. 1900s.

91 - 12" Blown bud vase, ca. 1900s.

92 - 5" Pedestal clock, "Parker & Whipple Co., Meridan, Conn." ca. 1884.

93 - Tambour Art Clock by McKee, c.1923-1925. See *Complete Book of McKee Glass*; Stout; 1972; pg. 97, illustrated pg. 107.

94 - Hobnail Relish dish on wheels, ca. 1870s.

95 - 4" compote. The pattern is Bag , #800 by George Duncan & Sons, ca. 1892. See *Early Duncan Glassware*; Bredehoft-Fogg-Maloney; pg. 73.

96 - Creamer in pattern #96 by Geo. Duncan & Sons, ca. 1887. The handle was applied by hand. See *Early Duncan Glassware*; Bredehoft-Fogg-Maloney; pg. 97.

97 - Genesta wall sconce by Bryce Bros., ca.1889. See *Victorian Colored Pattern Glass # 5*; Heacock, pg.80. It has been reproduced.

98 - 2$^{1}/_{2}$" Flower frog.

99 - 3$^{1}/_{2}$" Flower frog.

100 - 5" Apothecary bottle. Unmarked, ca. 1900s.

101 - 5" tall rose bowl, ca. 1890s.

102 - Flower frog over bowl, ca. 1900s.

103 - Silver hinged-top smelling salts bottle, ca. 1880s.

104 - Cut perfume bottle with cut stopper 12" tall, ca. 1860s.

105 - Cut perfume with cut stopper. 4" tall, ca. 1870s.

106 - Cut cologne with cut stopper, 5" tall, ca. 1870s.

107 - 4-bottle Caster Set in silverplate table-shaped holder. Tufts, ca. 1880s.

108 - 6-bottle Caster Set in silverplated bailer. Meriden, ca. 1880s.

109 - The Shell & Tassel bowl was designed and patented by Augustus H. Heisey, partner and son-in-law of Geo. Duncan, at the original Geo. Duncan & Sons glass factory. Mounted in silver-plated holder. Meriden, ca. 1880s.

110 - Pickle Caster. Daisy & Button insert. Meriden, ca. 1880s.

111 - Pickle Caster. Pressed Diamond insert, ca. 1880s.

112 - Silver-plated covered dish. Daisy & Button with Crossbars was made by Richards & Hartley, ca. 1885; See *Early American Pattern Glass 1850-1910*; Jenks & Luna; 1990; Wallace-Homestead; pg. 155.

113 - Bon bon dish. Fine cut. Silverplated under-plate and top. Loop finial, ca. 1890s.

114 - Triangular bowl with Tufts silver-plated holder. The glass insert is Daisy & Button with Thin Bars, made by Gillinder, ca. 1885. Early authors referred to it as Triangle.

115 - Spigot decanter with four shot glasses held in nickle-plated holder with turning windmill, ca. early 1900s.

116 - Celery vase Pressed Diamond set in Reed & Barton silver-plated holder, ca. 1880s.

117 - Marmalade/Jam Set Cross Bock in nickle-plated holder, ca. early 1900s.

118 - Glass celery boat. Daisy and Button or Octagon Rosette by Geo. Duncan & Sons, ca. 1884. See *Early Duncan Glassware*; Bredehoft-Fogg-Maloney; pg. 76. Reed and Barton holder.

119 - The pattern on the glass insert is Daisy & Button with Thumbprint Panels by Adams & Co., ca. 1886. See *Early American Pattern Glass 1850-1910*, Jenks & Luna; 1990; Wallace-Homestead; pg. 159. Reed and Barton holder.

120 - Spigot dispenser satin finish in brass holder with six matching satin finish tumblers. Hand-painted flowers on dispenser, ca. 1920s.

121 - Blown pinch bottle, 22" tall, ca. 1920s.

122 - Pair etched and cut vases. Bohemian, ca. 1890s.

123 - Mold blown fish bowl, 10" diameter, 2" tall, Signed GB, Gillinder and Bennett, ca. 1867.

124 - 16" tall kerosene lamp. Two Panel. Richards & Hartley, ca. 1880s. See *Oil Lamps*, Thuro, pg. 232.

125 - Tobacco humidor bowl/tray. Signed U.S. Glass Co., ca. 1891.

126 - Brass lamp, 8" tall. Stippled Loop shade, ca. 1890s.

127 - Blown small vase, 3½" tall, ca. 1860s.

128 - Tobacco/cigar humidor. Brass top. Daisy and Button . U.S. Glass Co., ca. 1890s.

129 - Aquarius lamp, U.S. Glass, ca. 1893. See "*Oil Lamps*, Thuro, pgs. 215, 315; 322.

130 - Cut glass perfume bottle, 7" tall. Cut glass stopper.

131 - Etched 3" candlestick. Cambridge, ca. 1920s.

132 - 2½" tall tumblers made by the Cambridge Glass Co., ca. 1934. See *The Cambridge Glass Co. 1930-1934, Cambridge, Ohio*. National Cambridge Collectors; pg. 34-16.

133 - Spooner, ca. 1900. National Star made for National Glass at the Riverside Glass Works. It may also be found with a ruby stain. See *Riverside Glass Works*; Gorham; pgs. 197-199.

134 - Blown bud vase. 5" tall, ca. 1890s.

135 - Cut glass covered jewel case 2½" x 3". Fresco motif, ca. 1920s. French.

136 - Cut glass inkwell 2½" x 2½" hinged lid, ca. 1900s.

137 - Pressed advertising inkwell 2½" x 2½" "Compliments of John M. Huiskamp" on lid, ca. 1900s.

138 - Cruet in the Ellrose pattern, made by Geo. Duncan & Sons, ca. 1885. See *Early Duncan Glassware*; Bredehoft-Fogg-Maloney; pg. 88.

139 - Lightning Jar 38" tall Quack Cure "Whiz Bang." Ca. 1890s.

140 - Cruet in Finecut pattern, probably made by Bryce. It appears to match the pattern shown in *Victorian Colored Pattern Glass #5*, Heacock and Bickenheuser.

141 - Salt shaker 2³/₄" tall, zinc top. Pressed Diamond. Central Glass, ca. 1888.

142 - Double salter, zinc handle/holder, ca. 1870s.

143 - Salt shaker 3¹/₂" tall. Pointed zinc tops, ca. 1870s. Rare in Vaseline.

144 - Butter dish, missing its lid. Lorne pattern by Bryce Bros. See *Victorian Colored Pattern Glass #5*; Heacock;1978; pg.82.

145 - Serpentine tray 8" long. Dewey. Indiana Tumbler and Goblet, ca. 1898.

146 - Handled candlestick. 4" tall.

147 - Serpentine tray. 10" long. Dewey. Indiana Tumbler and Goblet, ca. 1898.

148 - Opalescent atomizer. The patent for the hardware was issued to DeVilbiss in 1940. Fenton first began producing for DeVilbiss about 1940.

149 - Opalescent vase. 7¹/₂" tall, c. early 1900s.

150 - Opalescent milk pitcher. Diamond Spearhead, Dugan. ca. early 1900s.

151 - Opalescent tray 10" diameter. Beatty Swirl, Beatty & Sons, ca. 1880s.

152 - According to Heacock, Daisy & Fern in yellow Opalescent is not Victorian, therefore, this barber bottle would be Fenton. This piece was reproduced by Fenton for L.G. Wright in the 60s and 70s. See *Victorian Colored Pattern Glass #9*; Heacock, pg. 47.

153 - Opalescent Corn vase, Dugan, ca. 1905. Also reproduced for L.G. Wright by Fenton, however, this one is Dugan. See *Victorian Colored Pattern Glass #2*, Heacock, pg. 96.

154 - 6¹/₄" Topaz Opalescent Hobnail vase. Made by Fenton from 1941-43 (ware #389) and in 1959-62 (ware #3956). (F.A.G.C.A. price guides)

155 - Topaz Opalescent Hobnail salt shaker (ware #389). Made by Fenton in 1941-43. (F.A.G.C.A. price guides)

156 - Opalescent wine glass. Moon & Star. Many companies made this pattern. This one is probably an L.G. Wright reproduction.

157 - Opalescent bud vase in silverplate holder, ca. 1898.

158 - Flower bowl or open sugar in Button Panels by Northwood, ca. 1899. See *Victorian Colored Pattern Glass #2*, Heacock, pg. 63, illustrated, pg. 83.

159 - Opalescent covered sugar. Fluted Scrolls, Northwood, ca. 1898. (See #160.)

160 - Opalescent creamer. Fluted Scrolls, Northwood, ca. 1898. Although some collectors refer to this pattern as Fluted Scrolls, most prefer the OMN (Original Manufacturer's Name) of Klondyke.

161 - Opalescent candy dish in Opal Open, Northwood, ca. 1910. It is also known as Beaded Panel. Fenton reproduced this pattern for L.G. Wright. See *Victorian Colored Pattern Glass #2*, Heacock, pg. 69, illus. pg. 85.

162 - Opalescent cake dish. Swirl, ca. 1920s.

163 - Opalescent Hobnail dish, 2¹/₂" tall by 6" diameter. It could be a butter dish minus its lid, produced by Hobbs, Brockunier & Co. and shown in *Victorian Colored Pattern Glass #2*, Heacock, pg. 35. Fenton made a Topaz Opalescent Hobnail candy jar from 1959-62 (ware # 3883). It is a copy of the original Hobbs piece. (F.A.G.C.A. price guides)

164 - Opalescent card receiver. Nautilus, by Northwood, ca. 1899. It is signed Northwood, in script. See *Victorian Colored Pattern Glass #2*, Heacock, pg. 18.

165 - Opalescent tumbler, ca. 1950s for L.G. Wright. Wright called the pattern Fern. It is pictured in an undated Wright catalogue.

166 - Opalescent sugar shaker in Spanish Lace, Northwood and National Glass. Not reproduced in tableware by Fenton. See *Victorian Colored Pattern Glass #9*; Heacock;1987, pg. 61.

167 - Opalescent sugar shaker made by Fenton for L.G. Wright. (FMF)

168 - Opalescent cruet made by Fenton for L.G. Wright. Northwood did not make Daisy & Fern in Vaseline. The cruet is pictured in an undated Wright catalogue. The cruet is missing its stopper. See explanation for #152.

169 - Opalescent creamer in Twist pattern. Advertised in 1901. See *Victorian Colored Pattern Glass #2*; Heacock; pgs. 64, 103.

170 - Topaz Opalescent 3$^{1/2}$" miniature hand vase made by Fenton from 1941-43. See *Fenton Glass: 2nd 25 Yrs.*; Heacock; 1980; pgs. 53, 64 & 103.

171- Swan vase, probably made by Diamond in the 1920s. (FMF)

172 - Opalescent spooner. Brideshead. English, ca. 1900s.

173 - Opalescent bud vase in silverplate holder. Mold blown English.

174 - Opalescent 11" chalice. Claw feet. Iris. English, ca. 1890s.

175 - Pair of French seltzer bottles, ca. 1920s.

176 - Swedish jewel box, hand-painted flowers. Bronze trim, ca. 1900s.

177 - Pair of French cologne burners, ca. 1890.

178 - Opalescent stripe sweetmeat dish in silver-plated holder, ca. 1890.

179 - Bohemian (Czech) cologne bottle, matching stopper, gold trim, ca. 1888.

180 - Queen's Crown is English glass, ca. 1898-1899. See Heacock's *Collecting Glass*, Vol.1, p. 35.

181 - Opalescent canoe dish. 7$^{1/2}$", War of the Roses. English, ca. 1890s.

182 - Opalescent canoe dish. 9$^{1/2}$", War of the Roses. English, ca. 1890s.

183 - Opalescent boat on wheels. English, ca. 1900.

184 - Opalescent 3-pointed star dish, War of the Roses, ca. 1890s.

185 - Opalescent 4-pointed star dish, War of the Roses, ca. 1890s.

186 - Perfume 2" x 2" barrel, English, ca. 1860.

187 - Opalescent finger salt, silverplated base. English, ca. 1890s.

188 - Opalescent sweetmeat dish in handled silverplate holder. English, ca. 1890s.

189 - Opalescent 3-handled salt. English, ca. 1880s.

190 - Pair of neo-classical handled urns. U.S. Glass Co., ca. 1900.

191 - Scalloped oval dish in spelter holder, ca. 1900.

192 - Notched spoonholder on nickle-plated base. English, ca. 1900.

193 - Triangular vase. 7$^{1/2}$" tall. Half Art Nouveau, half Art Deco pattern. English, ca. 1925.

194 - Russian tea glass, ca. 1885.

195 - Queen Victoria coronation statuette. English, ca. 1869.

196 - Bohemian cut covered dish with underplate, ca. 1890s.

197, 198 - Heavily cut glass covered mug with gold finial and underplate. English, ca. 1880s.

199 - Swan flower holder. English. Webb & Hammond, 1874.

200 - Bee honey pot. English. Mappin & Webb. ca. 1900.

201 - Czech chameleon necklace, ca. 1935.

202 - French Valerysthal figural toothpick holder.

203 - Italian egg paperweight with red center and pedestal, ca. 1930s.

204 - Opalescent 20" vase. Ribbed Spiral. Model Flint Glass, ca. 1902.

205 - Opalescent open compote. Closed base. Opal Open pattern. Northwood, ca. 1910. See explanation for #161.

206 - Opalescent 8¼" vase.

207 - Opalescent 10" tall Fenton commemorative convention vase, ca. 1960s.

208 - Opalescent 13" tall vase. Ribbed spiral Model Flint Glass, ca. 1902.

209 - Opalescent hexagonal plate. Cambridge, ca. 1920s.

210 - Opalescent rose bowl. Opal Open. Northwood, ca. 1910. See explanation for #161.

211, 215 - Topaz Opalescent Hobnail. It was made by Fenton from 1941-43. See *Fenton*

Glass: 2nd 25 Yrs.; Heacock; 1980; Antique Publications, pg.73. Dewdrop was Imperial's line and the name was never used by Fenton.

212 - Opalescent 4" vase. Lattice Spiral.

213 - Opalescent rose bowl. Jacqueline. Fenton, ca. 1960s.

214 - Opalescent hanging spoon sweetmeat dish in silverplate holder. English, ca. 1900.

215 - Topaz Opalescent Hobnail compote. See #211.

216 - Opalescent barber bottle pictured in an undated L.G. Wright catalogue. Wright called it Rib.

217 - Topaz Opalescent Horizontal Rib atomizer, made by Fenton for DeVilbiss, probably 1940-41.

218 - Opalescent Daisy and Button toothpick, ca. 1930s.

219 - Topaz Opalescent Hobnail slipper, made by Fenton from 1941-43 (ware #389) and 1959-62 (ware #3995). (F.A.G.C.A. price guides)

220 - Topaz Opalescent Hobnail miniature cornucopia candlestick was made by Fenton from 1941-43 (ware #389). Although other colors were made after 1952, the candlestick was not made again in topaz. (F.A.G.C.A. price guides)

221 - Opalescent basket. 5" tall. Taylor. Special order by Fenton, ca. 1970s.

222 - Opalescent eye cup, ca. 1970s.

223 - Topaz Opalescent fairy light produced by Fenton for A.A. Importing Co. in 1970 (ware #3608). (F.A.G.C.A. price guides)

224 - This opalescent high shoe was never made by Fenton. It was first made by Mosser in 1973.

225 - Iridescent Stretch glass 8$\frac{1}{2}$" candlestick made by Fenton, ca. 1920s. (FMF)

226 - Iridescent taffeta 10" covered candy dish. Fenton, ca. 1920s.

227 - Iridescent stretch 12" bowl. German silver edge trim. Bernard Rice & Son, ca. 1924.

228 - Iridescent stretch 10" tall candlestick. Fenton, ca. 1926.

229 - Stain finish 9" tall vase. Hand-painted flowers, ca. 1928.

230 - Iridescent stretch 8" diameter basket. German silver handle and edge trim, ca. 1924.

231 - Satin finish 7" candlestick, ca. 1928.

232 - Satin finish "Bath-a-Sweet" commercial bottle, 7$\frac{1}{2}$" tall, ca. 1936.

233, 234 - Acid-etched covered candy dish and vase in the Jack Frost pattern by Tiffin Glass Co., ca. 1930. See *Tiffin Glass*; Piña and Gallagher; 1996; illustrated pgs. 61 & 62.

235 - Satin finish 5" tall powder jar. Figural top, ca. 1932.

236 - Satin hen on next covered bowl, ca. 1960s.

237 - Iridescent taffeta handled mint server in Meriden silver holder, ca. 1891.

238 - Iridescent taffeta 6$\frac{1}{2}$" diameter plate, ca. 1909.

239 - Stretch 4" tall powder jar. Bronze filigree and inset stones over top, ca. 1931.

240 - Satin finish creamer Hobb's Hobnail, ca. 1890.

241 - Satin finish talc flask. Art Deco Sunrise pattern brass top and screen, ca. 1935.

242 - Stretch 12" plate with gilt edging, Fenton, ca. 1926.

243 - Satin candlestick in Roses. Made by the U.S. Glass Co. See *Tiffin Glass*; Piña and Gallagher; 1996; illustrated pg. 132.

244 - Stretch 14" platter, black edging Fenton, ca. 1922.

245 - Stretch 10" bowl, Fenton, ca. 1926.

246 - Stretch retroverted bowl, ca. 1928.

247 - Stretch 8" covered candy dish, ca. 1927.

248 - Stretch 7$\frac{3}{4}$" diameter bowl, ca. 1930.

249 - Stretch 4$\frac{3}{4}$" diameter bowl, ca. 1928.

250 - 3$\frac{1}{2}$" tall Stretch candlestick made by Fenton. (FMF)

251 - Stretch bonbon dish, Fenton, ca. 1926.

252 - Stretch octagonal plate, 7$\frac{3}{4}$", ca. 1928.

253 - Stretch raised shallow bowl, 10" diameter. Northwood, ca. 1926.

254 - Stretch "tumble up," Fenton, ca. 1922.

255 - Satin finish 11$\frac{1}{2}$" diameter, ca. 1935.

256 - Stretch 7$\frac{1}{4}$" diameter bowl on swirl pedestal, ca. 1932.

257 - Stretch 7" tall reversible candlestick/chalice. Possibly made by the U.S. Glass Co. (FMF)

258 - Stretch 8" diameter open compote Northwood, ca. 1922.

259 - Stretch 8" diameter bowl. Fenton, ca. 1926.

260 - Stretch 6" diameter bowl. Northwood, ca. 1926.

261 - Stretch 6½" diameter bowl. Fenton, ca. 1928.

262 - Stretch 6" tall glass covered compote. Fenton. (FMF)

263 - Stretch cone-shaped bowl, ca. 1928.

264 - Ash tray/matchbox holder. 5" diameter, ca. 1926.

265 - Stretch pedestal dish, 2" tall, 6" diameter. Fenton, ca. 1928.

266 - Stretch mayonnaise server. Fenton, ca. 1926.

267 - Stretch mayonnaise cup. Fenton, ca. 1926.

268 - Stretch mayonnaise scoop. Fenton, ca. 1926.

269 - Stretch 9" plate. Fenton, 1921.

270 - Satin finish vase, 10" tall. Handpainted flowers, ca. 1936.

271 - Flared 10" tall bud vase.

272 - Straight 10" tall bud vase.

273 - Octagonal 7" plate with design around edge, ca. 1934.

274 - Loving cup vase. Fostoria, ca. 1927.

275 - Square covered container. Fostoria, ca. 1927.

276 - Buddha. Cambridge, ca. 1926.

277 - Automotive bud vase. Flair-top, ca. 1927.

278 - Automotive bud vase, narrow top, ca. 1929.

279 - Fluted beer mug.

280-A - Stretch flat top vase. Fenton, ca. 1928.

280-B - Underplate, 8½" diameter.

281 - Baccarat relish dish, ca. 1930s.

282, 283 - Covered etched candy dish. Cambridge, ca. 1927.

284 - Flair top mug.

285 - The etched pattern is Majestic or #732 by Cambridge. See *Cambridge Glass Co.*; National Cambridge Collectors; Pgs. 28, 56.

286 - Bud vase, 12" tall, ca. 1934.

287 - Crackled covered pitcher, 6½" tall, and matching tumbler, ca. 1935.

288 - Controlled bubble console set. Pair 12" tall candlesticks and flared 8" tall vase. Pairpoint, ca. 1937.

289 - Blown crackle pinch pitcher and matching cups, ca. 1935.

290 - Etched atomizer 8" tall. Labeled "T.J. Holmes & Co. Boston", ca. 1923.

291 - Iridescent covered cookie jar. Cherry and Cable. Westmoreland, ca. 1960s.

292 - Double handled covered cookie jar. Handpainted Plantation. Westmoreland, ca. 1960s.

293 - Cat figural covered dish. Westmoreland, ca. 1958.

294 - Creamer and sugar. Handpainted Plantation. Westmoreland, ca. 1960s.

295 - Duck figural covered dish. Westmoreland, ca. 1958.

296 - 5" Candlestick. Fostoria, ca. 1927.

297 - Perfume set included two turban top perfumes. Combination perfume/powder jar and oval tray, ca. 1935.

298 - Mold blown heavily bubbled vase. 12" tall and 8" wide.

299 - Scalloped bowl is McKee's "1776 Colonial" pattern, c.1920s. See *Complete Book of McKee Glass*; Stout; 1972; pg.116, illustrated pg. 107.

300 - Art deco cruet. Flat stopper, ca. 1938.

301 - Art deco dresser tray, ca. 1935.

302 - Beaded Block square dish. Made by Imperial Glass, ca. 1927-1930s.

303 - Triangular ash tray/matchbox holder, ca. 1932.

304, 305, 306 - Sherbet, round plate, and octagonal plate in L.E. Smith's By Cracky pattern. See *Colored Glassware of the Depression Era 2*; Weatherman; 1974; pg. 315.

307 - Reamer, horizontal handle, ca. 1930s.

308 - Sectioned candy dish in handled nickel plate holder, ca. 1930s.

309 - Advertising covered candy dish "Keep filled With Paul Smiths candies."

310 - Teaberry Gum tray, ca. 1928.

311 - Retroverted Bowl console set, ca. 1935.

312 - Footed bowl, 8" diameter, 6" tall. Pebbly grain, ca. 1928.

313 - Green Depression (Green Vaseline) covered jewel box. French.

314 - Green Depression (Green Vaseline) apothecary jar.

315 - Green Depression (Green Vaseline) "Heinz 57 Varieties" pickle dish.

316 - Green Depression (Green Vaseline) Square bowl in spatter holder.

317 - Green Depression (Green Vaseline) Frigidaire bottle.

318 - Square 9$\frac{1}{4}$" tall vase. Nude on four sides. Semi-satin finish, ca. 1920.

319 - Square 10$\frac{1}{2}$" tall vase. Bubble design, ca. 1930s.

320 - Console set 8" tall scalloped bowl, pair of 6" candlesticks. Viking, ca. 1950s.

321 - Opalescent mold blown fish dated "1982 Gibson."

322 - Fish bowl. 12" diameter, 7" tall, ca. 1937.

323 - Fish card tray. 6" long, ca. 1935.

324 - Art nouveau fish bowl on bronze wash stand with seahorses, ca. 1926.

325 - Art deco fish bowl on bronze wash stand with dolphins, ca. 1936.

326 - Goblet 7" tiered pattern. Green base, ca. 1932.

327 - Covered pitcher, 9$\frac{1}{2}$" tall, light flute. Applied green handle, ca. 1929.

328 - Sherbet light flute. Green base, ca. 1929.

329 - Wine glass, 5" tall, light flute. Green base, 1927.

330 - Goblet 5" tall, light flute. Green base, ca. 1929.

331 - Goblet 6" tall, light flute. Green base, ca.1929.

332 - Long stem goblet, 7$\frac{1}{2}$" tall. Green base, ca. 1929.

333 - Vase 8$\frac{1}{2}$" tall. Green base, ca. 1929.

334 - Handled goblet. Blue handle (applied), blue base, ca. 1938. Probably not Fenton. (FMF)

335 - Sherbet 4" tall. Swirl, tiered stem, ca. 1937.

336 - Dessert 4" tall, light flute. Green base, ca. 1929.

337 - Champagne light flute, 5" tall. Green base, 1929.

338 - Plate 8$\frac{1}{2}$" diameter, ca. 1929.

339 - Small bulbous glass, 3" tall, ca. 1935.

340 - 4" tall glass. Cambridge, ca. 1935. See explanation for #132.

341 - Tumblers, 5" tall, ca. 1935.

342 - Dolphin candlestick, square indented base. Viking, ca. 1980.

343 - Chick on two-handled basket, 5" tall. Westmoreland mold mark. Reissued in Vaseline by Summit Art Glass, ca. 1980.

344 - Swan by Summit Art Glass. The original Westmoreland mold had glass in the neck opening.

345 - Kneeling Bactrian camel. Reissued in Vaseline by Summit Art Glass, ca. 1980.

346 - "Atterbury" Rabbit. Imperial mold mark. Reissued in Vaseline by Summit Art glass, ca. 1980.

347 - Hen on nest, 6" long x 4" tall. Mosser, ca. 1970.

348 - Lamb figural, 2-piece dish. 5" long x 4" tall. Degenhart, ca. 1970.

349 - Elephant on stand, 5" x 5". Viking, 1980.

350 - Erect rabbit, 7"tall. Viking, 1974.

351 - Robin on nest, 5" long x 4" tall. Degenhart, 1976.

352 - Turkey on nest, 5" long x 4: tall. Degenhart, ca. 1975.

353 - Rooster on nest, 5" long x 4" tall. Westmoreland mold mark. Reissued in Vaseline by Summit Art Glass, ca. 1980.

354 - Small sitting dog with collar, 2" tall. Westmoreland mold mark. Reissued in Vaseline by Viking, ca. 1980s.

355 - Owl on books, 3" tall. Degenhart, ca. 1969.

356 - Scotty candy container, 3" tall. Made in Vaseline. S. Grossett Co., ca. 1940.

357 - Mini hen on nest 2$\frac{1}{2}$" long x 2" tall. Summit Art Glass, ca. 1980.

358 - Small hen on nest 3$\frac{1}{2}$" long x 3" tall. Summit Art Glass, ca. 1980s.

359 - Perched bird 3" long x 1$\frac{1}{2}$" tall. Mosser, ca. 1970s.

360 - Kitten, 2$\frac{1}{2}$" tall. Boyd, ca. 1980s.

361 - Seated dog, open base 3" tall. Originally candy container. Degenhart, ca. 1970s.

362 - Small rabbit, 3$\frac{1}{2}$" long x 1$\frac{1}{2}$" tall. Viking, ca. 1975.

363 - Unicorn, 3$\frac{1}{4}$" tall. Boyd, ca. 1980s.

364 - Horse, 4$\frac{1}{4}$" tall. Boyd, ca. 1980s.

365 - Pony, 5$\frac{3}{4}$" tall. New Martinsville-Viking Mosser mold mark, ca. 1960s.

366 - Frog. Viking, ca. 1970.

367 - Sitting rabbit, 4" long x 5½" tall. Viking, ca. 1975.

368 - "Bashful Charlotte" flower frog. 10¼" tall. Reissued in Vaseline, ca. 1980s.

369 - "Cambridge Lady" lamp base. 8" tall. Reissued in Vaseline, ca. 1980s.

370 - "Priscilla" doll, 5½" tall. Degenhart, ca. 1960.

371 - "Cat on Hamper" covered dish. Summit Art Glass Co.

372 - "Santa Claus Bell," ca. 1980s.

373 - Banjo ashtray, ca. 1960s.

374 - Violin ashtray, ca. 1960s.

375 - Miniature candelabra. Westmoreland, ca. 1960.

376 - Miniature piano covered candy dish. Mosser, ca. 1960.

377 - Children's punch bowl set with six cups. Fish and flower pattern. Viking, ca. 1960.

378 - Children's punch bowl set with six cups. Fan pattern. Westmoreland, ca. 1960.

379 - Bottoms Up shot glass, ca. 1980. (Reissued in Vaseline.)

380, 381 - Lacy butter pats, 2" diameter. Swirl & Eagle designs. Millville Glass, ca. 1980.

382 - Ballerina dish 8¾" long. Westmoreland mold mark on foot. Reissued in Vaseline, ca. 1980s.

383 - Children's pitcher, 2" tall. Degenhart, ca. 1960s.

384 - Children's potty. Degenhart, ca. 1960s.

385 - Sugar and creamer. Fan pattern. Westmoreland, ca. 1980s.

386 - Elizabeth Degenhart 5" diameter plate. Degenhart, ca. 1975.

387 - Master salt and individual salt. The Cane pattern was made by Gillinder & Sons and McKee & Bros., ca. 1875-1885.

388 - Heart and lyre plate, 3" diameter. Degenhart, ca. 1970.

389 - Starfish coaster, 3" diameter. Degenhart, ca. 1970.

390 - Children's bordered butter dish. Strawberry pattern. Inscription reads "Souvenir Coney Island, 1906," but is really a reissue in Vaseline, ca. 1970s.

391 - Seal of Ohio plate, 3" diameter. Degenhart, ca. 1970.

392 - Hatching chick tray. Westmoreland moldmark. Reissued in Vaseline by Summit Art Glass, ca. 1980s.

393 - "Mosser Glass" paperweight, ca. 1970s.

394 - "Boyd Crystal Art Glass" paperweight, ca. 1980s.

395 - Heart-shaped toothpick holder. Reissued by Boyd in Vaseline in 1991.

396 - Bicentennial Liberty Bell "1976", Degenhart.

397, 398 - Children's water set pitcher and six glasses. Heron pattern. Viking, ca. 1960s.

399 - "End" clown. Mosser, ca. 1985.

400 - "Quinn" clown on barrel. Mosser, 1982.

401 - "Jiggs" clown with balloons. Mosser, 1981.

402 - Heart covered jewel box. Degenhart, ca. 1970s.

403 - Miniature dollhouse pitcher, 1" tall, ca. 1955.

404 - Basket, 7" tall. Westmoreland, ca. 1960s.

405 - Pitcher with reamer cover, 7" tall. Lemon & Orange embossing. Reissued in Vaseline by Summit, ca. 1980s.

406 - Basket, 9½" tall.

407 - Measuring cup with reamer top, 5" tall. Reissued in Vaseline by Summit, ca. 1980s.

408 - Sundae dish. Strawberry and grapes, ca. 1960s.

409 - Whiskey flask. MMA (Metropolitan Museum of Art) reissue, ca. 1970s.

410 - Flip glass MMA reissue. Diamond Band, ca. 1970s.

411 - Covered sugar 5" tall. Starburst pinwheel, ca. 1970s.

412 - Reamer vertical handle. Reissued in Vaseline by Summit, ca. 1980s.

413 - Spoon rest, 7½" x 2", ca. 1955.

414 - Fairy lamp with handle, 5¼" tall. Holly pattern, ca. 1960s.

415 - Fairy lamp. Daisy & Button, 6" tall, ca. 1960s.

416 - Covered butter, 6" Cherry and Cable, ca. 1970s.

417 - Children's cake plate with Westmoreland mark. Reissued in Vaseline by Summit, ca. 1980s.

418 - Children's banana dish. Westmoreland mold mark. Reissued in Vaseline by Summit, ca. 1980s.

419 - Handled mirror. Boyd, ca. 1980s.

420 - Hand card tray. Reissue of Art Nouveau mold in Vaseline, ca. 1970.

421 - Knife support, ca. 1960.

422 - Dolphin covered dish. Kemple reissue in Vaseline, ca. 1965.

423 - Doll holding rabbit. Mosser, ca. 1960.

424 - Measuring cup. Depression mold reissued in Vaseline, ca. 1980s.

425 - Children's cup. Heron pattern.

426 - Children's cup. Dog and Cat pattern.

427 - Children's cup. Alphabet.

428 - Party favor 4" basket. Tiffin, ca. 1930s. See *Tiffin Glass*; Piña and Gallagher; 1996; illus. pg. 11.

429 - "Duboe" Stick handle reamer. Reissued in Vaseline, ca. 1980s.

430 - Degenhart Hatchet, 7½" long, ca. 1970s.

431 - Ashtray, 3" diameter, ca. 1957.

432 - The pressed Diamond celery vase in the center is in a Reed & Barton silverplated holder, ca. 1880s. The two etched and cut vases are Bohemian, ca. 1890s.

433 - French seltzer (Vichy) bottles, one posed horizontally to show the etching.

434 - Triangular Daisy & Button banquet bowl in elaborate Tuft's silver holder, ca. 1890.

435 - Stretch glass mayonnaise set, Fenton Art Glass Co., ca. 1926.

436 - Assortment of perfume bottles and atomizers; the center item doubles as a powder jar. From left: etched atomizer, 8" tall, labeled "T.V. Holmes & Co., Boston," ca. 1923; turban top perfume, ca. 1935; combination perfume/powder jar, ca. 1935; flat top perfume, ca. 1935; and opalescent atomizer, DeVilbiss, ca. 1928.

437 - A group of Vaseline articles seen just as the human eye views them, in natural light. The phrase "easy on the eyes" is an actuality here, since yellow-green is exactly in the center of the human eye's spectrum.

438 - Palm Beach pattern covered sugar bowl, attributed to the United States Glass Co. by Heacock, ca. 1905.

439 - Palm Beach pattern creamer, attributed to the United States Glass Co. by Heacock, ca. 1905.

440 - Palm Beach pattern covered butterdish, attributed to the United States Glass Co. by Heacock, ca. 1905.

441 - Palm Beach pattern spooner, attributed to the United States Glass Co. by Heacock, ca. 1905.

442 - Palm Beach pattern tumbler, attributed to the United States Glass Co. by Heacock, ca. 1905.

443 - Palm Beach pattern pitcher, attributed to the United States Glass Co. by Heacock, ca. 1905.

444 - Palm Beach pattern sauce, attributed to the United States Glass Co. by Heacock, ca. 1905.

445 - Palm Beach pattern bowl, attributed to the United States Glass Co. by Heacock, ca. 1905.

446 - Cactus pattern goblet in Topaz Opalescent. Fenton Art Glass Co., ca. 1959.

447 - Cactus pattern footed nut dish in Topaz Opalescent. Fenton Art Glass Co., ca. 1959.

448 - Cactus pattern candleholder in Topaz Opalescent. Fenton Art Glass Co., ca. 1959.

449 - Cactus pattern 7" basket in Topaz Opalescent. Fenton Art Glass Co., ca. 1959.

450 - Cactus pattern 6" fan vase in Topaz Opalescent. Fenton Art Glass Co., ca. 1959.

451 - Cactus pattern salt shaker in Topaz Opalescent. Fenton Art Glass Co., ca. 1959.

452 - Cactus pattern cruet with stopper in Topaz Opalescent. Fenton Art Glass Co., ca. 1959.

453 - Cactus pattern banana bowl in Topaz Opalescent. Fenton Art Glass Co., ca. 1959.

454 - Cactus pattern handled bonbon in Topaz Opalescent. Fenton Art Glass Co., ca. 1959.

455 - Cactus pattern covered sugar in Topaz Opalescent. Fenton Art Glass Co., ca. 1959.

456 - Cactus pattern creamer in Topaz Opalescent. Fenton Art Glass Co., ca. 1959.

457 - Cactus pattern 1/4 lb. covered butterdish in Topaz Opalescent. Fenton Art Glass Co., ca. 1959.

Author's note: On page 79, "Which of these isn't Vaseline?" the Vaseline piece on the right doesn't appear anywhere else and was not identified in the original edition. This Hobnail 4-footed creamer was made by the La Belle Glass Co., ca. 1886. See *Harry Northwood: The Early Years 1881-1900*, Heacock, Measell, and Wiggins, illustrated on page 15.

458 - Opalescent pitcher. Klondyke/Fluted Scrolls, with gilt trim and enameled band of Daisies. Northwood, ca. 1897.

459 - Opalescent striped Bride's basket with cranberry ruffle, in silver-plated holder.

460 - Opalescent novelty vase. Concave Columns. Dugan, ca. 1901.

461 - Butter dish, 1/4 lb., 4" diameter. Dewey. Indiana Tumbler & Goblet, ca. 1900.

462 - Opalescent Rose bowl. Spanish Lace. Northwood, ca. 1899.

463 - Opalescent celery vase with cranberry edging. Northwood Block. Northwood, ca. 1905.

464 - Opalescent bowl, blown.

465 - Opalescent novelty bowl. Beaded Drapes. Northwood, ca. 1905.

466 - Opalescent shallow bowl. Heirloom. Fostoria, ca. 1960-62.

467 - Opalescent vase. Heirloom. Fostoria, ca. 1960-62.

468 - Opalescent flora candle bowl. Heirloom. Fostoria, ca. 1960-62.

469 - Opalescent candle vase. Heirloom. Fostoria, ca. 1960-61.

470 - Owl fairy lamp.

471 - Bowl. Peacock & Eye. Imperial for Metropolitan Museum of Art, ca. 1970s.

472 - Carnival glass bowl. Open Rose. Imperial.

473 - Opalescent divided relish dish. Sanibel. Duncan & Miller.

474 - Sandwich tray, gold design, fleur-de-lis handle. Riviera. Fostoria.

475 - Opalescent basket with notched cobalt blue handle. Lily of the Valley. Fenton, 1997.

476 - Opalescent vase. Atlantis. Fenton, 1997.

477 - Opalescent basket. Thumbprint. Fenton, ca. 1960s. The basket was not part of their line and was most likely a sample.

478 - Opalescent nut dish. Scroll. Fenton, 1997.

479 - Opalescent milk pitcher with reed handle. Fern. Fenton for L.G. Wright.

480 - Opalescent bud vase. Hobnail. Fenton.

481 - Opalescent butter dish. Fenton.

482 - Opalescent vase. Coinspot. Fenton, ca. 1940s.

483 - Opalescent footed dish. Daisy & Button. Fenton for L.G. Wright.

484 - Opalescent covered compote. Daisy & Button. Fenton for L.G. Wright.

485 - Compote, 6" tall, 8$^1/_2$" diameter. Thousand Eye. U.S. Glass, ca. 1891.

486 - Bowl, 2$^1/_2$" tall, 8" diameter Quilted Diamond. Maker unknown, ca. 1880s.

487 - Bowl, rectangular. Daisy & Button.

488 - Covered dish. Lattice & Thumbprint.

489 - Master fruit bowl, 9-ftd., 2$^1/_2$" tall, 6$^1/_2$" diameter. Ranson. Riverside Glass, ca. 1899.

490 - Spooner with gold decoration. Petticoat. Riverside Glass, ca. 1902.

491 - Platter, oval. Two Panel. Richards & Hartley, ca. 1891.

492 - Platter, oval, 2-handled. Daisy & Button.

493 - Relish dish, boat-shaped. Rose Sprig. Campbell, Jones & Co., ca. 1886.

494 - Star bowl. Hobbs & Brockunier.

495 - Toothpick with gold decoration. Ranson. Riverside Glass, ca. 1899.

496 - Egg cup. Daisy & Button.

497 - Open salt, oval. Two Panel. Richards & Hartley, ca. 1891.

498 - Sauce dish, ftd. Quilted Diamond. Maker unknown, ca. 1880s.

499 - Stretch cake plate, 9¹/₂" diameter, 27 panels with a distinct design in each panel, outer edge has a concentric circle. ca. 1920s.

500 - Stretch bowl with cut-out edges, referred to as "Leeds" in U.S. Glass advertisements. U.S. Glass, ca. 1925.

501 - Stretch plate, 9¹/₂" diameter, 27 panels, ca. 1920s.

502 - Stretch compote, 3³/₄" tall, 7" d. ca. 1920s.

503 - Stretch vase, 6" tall, 4¹/₂" diameter. Quilted Diamond.

504 - Stretch compote, 4¹/₂" tall, 6" diameter, ca. 1920s.

505 - Stretch bowl, 3¹/₄" tall, 9³/₄" diameter. 28 panels, ca. 1920s.

506 - Stretch compote with fluted panels, 4³/₄"tall, 9³/₄" diameter. Northwood/U.S. Glass, ca. 1920s.

507 - Stretch compote, 5¹/₂" tall, 7¹/₂" diameter, 21 panels, concentric circle around edge, ca. 1920s.

508 - Stretch cheese dish, 2¹/₂" tall, 4³/₄" diameter, ca. 1920s.

509 - Stretch compote with fluted panels, black enamel edging, 4" tall, 6¹/₂" diameter. Northwood/U.S. Glass, ca. 1920s.

510 - Engraved plate, wheel-cut. ca. 1920s.

511 - Engraved bud vase.

512 - Engraved plate, wheel-cut, octagonal. Possibly Cambridge, ca. 1920s.

513 - Engraved plate. 77 cut 9. Imperial Glass, ca. 1920s.

514 - Engraved dish, divided, wheel-cut. ca. 1920s.

515 - Engraved small compote.

516 - Engraved 3-pc. mayonnaise, wheel-cut. ca. 1920s.

517 - Engraved bowl, wheel-cut. Butterfly and flower design. ca. 1920s.

518 - Engraved compote, ftd., wheel-cut, floral design, ca. 1920s.

519 - Pitcher, panelled.

520 - Sherbet. Roulette. Hocking Glass, ca. 1935-39.

521 - Cruet, crystal handle, missing stopper. Corded Optic. Federal Glass, ca. 1926.

522 - Underplate, 15¹/₂" diameter. Twisted Optic. Imperial.

523 - Satin bowl with gold bands.

524 - Satin vase with enamel flowers.

525 - Satin votive.

526 - Satin saucer. Tiffin.

527 - Plate. Strawflower. Imperial, ca. 1920s.

528 - Plate. Lacy design with crackle-type center, 8$^1/_2$" diameter.

529 - Plate. Romanesque. L.E. Smith, ca. 1926.

530 - Compote, fluted.

531 - Covered candy dish.

532 - Carnival glass collector plate. Apollo 15. Wheaton, ca. 1971.

533 - Carnival glass collector plate. Rev. Billy Graham. Wheaton, ca. 1970s.

534 - Candleholders, fluted, pr.

535 - Bowl, double-fluted.

536 - Rose bowl, ftd. Probably European.

537 - Carnival glass boy/girl bookends. Kemple mould. Wheaton, ca. 1970s.

538 - Miniature lamp. Grape design. L.E. Smith, ca. 1980s.

539 - Sherbet, green foot, needle-etched.

540 - Vase.

541 - Goblet. Inverted Thumbprint. Indiana Tumbler.

542 - Tumbler. Tiffin.

543 - Goblet. Swirl.

544 - Perfume with enamel flowers.

545 - Jelly dish, 8", Twiggy. Indiana Glass, ca. 1920s.

546 - Champagne glasses, panelled, pair. Possibly Tiffin.

547 - Necklace.

548 - Opalescent goblet. Panel Grape.

549 - Mayonnaise.

550 - Ladle for #549.

551 - Vase. Lily of the Valley. Westmoreland mould.

552 - Candleholders, pair Westmoreland mould. Rosso.

553 - Butter dish. Swan. Westmoreland mould. Rosso.

554 - Covered dish. Horse.

555 - Salt & pepper. Cactus.

556 - Toothpick. Indian head. Rosso.

557 - Toy water set. Little Jo. Westmoreland.

558 - Assorted open salts. Rosso, ca. 1990s.

559 - Soup plate, sq. Thousand Eye.

560 - Sugar bowl. Texas.

561 - Toothpick. Strawberry.

562 - Large shoe with cat.

563 - Ashtray. Viking, ca. 1970s.

564 - ABC plate.

565 - Toothpick. Floral design. Summit.

566 - Opalescent miniature vase. Fenton, ca. 1940s.

567 - Opalescent Jack-in-the-pulpit. Gibson, 1997.

568 - Slag figurine. Melanie. Summit, ca. 1980s.

569 - Toothpick.

570 - Pin dish. Val St. Lambert.

571 - Carnival open salt, large duck. Westmoreland mould. Rosso.

572 - Open salt. Swan.

573 - Commemorative plate, small, illustrated. Francis G. Paul 33' class. Boyd.

574 - Rex the dinosaur. Boyd,1994.

575 - Tommy the tiger. Boyd.

576 - Chicken miniature. Signed "E.E."

577 - Toothpick. Daisy Button. Boyd,1991.

578 - Carnival Virgil the clown. Boyd,1994.

579 - Skippy the dog. Boyd, 1996.

580 - Jeremy the frog. Boyd, 1992.

581 - Nut dip. Candlewick. Boyd, 1988.

582 - Taxi. Boyd, 1994.

583 - Carnival Tractor. Boyd.

584 - Toothpick. Beaded Oval. Boyd, 1991.

585 - Carnival Airplane. Boyd.

586 - Carnival Candy the carousel horse. Boyd, 1994.

587 - Toothpick. Hoppy 3. Limited edition. Boyd, 1996.

588 - Nancy the miniature doll. Hand decorated for Christmas. Boyd, 1996.

589 - Opalescent Chicken salt. Boyd, 1980.

590 - Carnival Bunny salt. Boyd, 1988.

591 - Marble holder. Boyd.

592 - Marble.

593 - Satin duck salt. Boyd, 1991.

Factories Producing Vaseline Glass

Author's note: The following list is not complete, by any means. Many other factories produced vaseline glass and the omission of any particular company was not intentional. Any information on other factories producing vaseline glass would be welcomed.

A. A. IMPORTING - This company is located in St. Louis, Missouri. Glass is imported from countries like Korea.

ADAMS - Adams, Macklin & Co. was established in Pittsburgh, Pennsylvania in 1851. In 1861, it became Adams & Co. In 1891, it became Factory A in the U.S. Glass Co.

BAKEWELL, PEARS & CO. - It was founded in Pittsburgh, Pennsylvania in 1808 as Bakewell & Ensell. In 1844, it became Bakewell, Pears & Co. It was reorganized as Bakewell, Pears & Co., Ltd. in 1880 and sold in 1882. This was the first company in the U.S. to produce flint glass.

BEATTY - In 1845, the company was founded as Beatty & Stillman. It was originally located in Steubenville, OH. A.J. Beatty & Sons, of Tiffin, Ohio, became Factory R in the U.S. Glass Co. in 1891.

BELMONT - The Belmont Glass Works (1866-1890) was located in Bellaire, Ohio.

BOYD - (Firefly). Boyd's Crystal Art Glass Co. is located in Cambridge, Ohio. The company was established in 1978. It is one of the few companies producing vaseline glass at the present. Their miniature figurines are highly collectible. This was originally the Degenhart factory.

BRYCE - (canary). Bryce Brothers Co., founded in 1850, was located in Mt. Pleasant, Pennsylvania. It specialized in hand-blown stemware and stemware that was engraved, etched, cut, or decorated. It also had a line of baskets, vases, and accessory pieces. Bryce Brothers Co. became a part of the U.S. Glass Co. in 1891, known as Factory B.

BUTLER - (canary). A wholesale house. Excerpts from an 1890 Butler Brothers catalogue show several lamps, a water set, a toothpick, a salt shaker, and a caster set available in canary.

CAMBRIDGE - The Cambridge Glass Co. was established in Cambridge, Ohio in 1900 by National Glass. It was sold in 1907 when National Glass went bankrupt. The factory was closed in 1954 and the Imperial Glass Co. purchased the molds and the Cambridge name in 1960. It was noted for its cut crystal.

CAMPBELL, JONES, and CO. - Campbell, Jones, and Co. was established in Pittsburgh, Pennsylvania, in 1865. They made mostly pressed glass and were noted for their novelties.

CANTON - The Canton Glass Co. was located in Canton, Ohio. Established in 1883, the company was noted for its pressed and novelty items. In 1900, it became a part of the National Glass Co.

CENTRAL - (canary). Central Glass Works was located in Wheeling, West Virginia. Dating back to the 1860s, it became Factory O in the U.S. Glass Co. in 1891. Central Glass Works was noted for its cut and etched glass. It also had a line of canary satin glass. Central Glass also made novelty items, such as shoes. It closed in 1939.

CO-OPERATIVE FLINT - (canary). The Co-operative Flint Glass Co. was originally the Beaver Falls Co-operative Glass Co. Located in Beaver Falls, Pennsylvania, the name was changed in 1889. Co-operative Flint produced pressed tableware, gift items, novelties, drawer pulls and other glass objects in canary. The plant closed in 1937.

DEGENHART - The Degenharts founded the Crystal Art Glass Co. in 1947 in Cambridge, Ohio. The factory was sold to the Boyds after the death of Elizabeth Degenhart in 1978. It is currently in operation as Boyd's Crystal Art Glass Co.

DOYLE - Doyle & Co. was located in Pittsburgh, Pennsylvania. In 1891, it became a part of the U.S. Glass Co., known as Factory P.

DUGAN - Occupying the former Northwood factory, the Dugan Glass Co. was established in 1892 in Indiana, Pennsylvania. The company became the Diamond Glass Co. in 1913. It was destroyed by fire in 1931.

DUNCAN & MILLER - (Chartreuse). Established in Washington, Pennsylvania in 1892 under the name Geo. Duncan & Sons, it was incorporated in 1900 and renamed Duncan & Miller. It was noted for its pressed wares and novelty items. The plant closed in 1955.

FEDERAL - The Federal Glass Co. was located in Columbus, Ohio. It began in 1900, making pressed crystal wares. In the twenties, it was noted for its iridescent colors, as well as combining crystal and color. Springtime green was introduced in 1926 and was produced until 1936. In 1958, the company became a division of the Federal Paper Board Co.

FENTON - (topaz). Beginning as a decorating shop in Martins Ferry, Ohio, the Fenton Art Glass Co. began making glass in Williamstown, West Virginia in 1907. It produced mold-blown and pressed glassware, including opalescent and carnival glass. Vaseline was made by Fenton in the late 1930s. Hobnail was introduced in 1941 and was one of Fenton's most popular lines. In 1959, Cactus, Coin Dot, and Hobnail were produced. Vaseline made a brief come-back with Lily of the Valley and CollectiBells. Fenton is still in operation. Fenton was also one of the three main producers of stretch glass, from 1920-1927. Their line was called "Florentine." Fenton has a new line of Vaseline glass.

FOSTORIA - (canary). The Fostoria Glass Co. began in 1887 in Fostoria, Ohio. It was moved to Moundsville, West Virginia in 1891. Canary was produced from 1924-1927. The factory closed in 1986.

FRY - (canary). Henry Fry started his company in Rochester, Pennsylvania in 1901. The business went into receivership upon his death in 1929. In 1933, the factory was purchased by Libbey Glass. Fry was noted for the combination of colors, such as canary with cobalt.

GILLINDER - Gillinder & Sons was located in Greensburg, Pennsylvania. In 1891, it became Factory G in the U.S. Glass Co. Gillinder Glass still operates, now in Port Jervis, New York.

HEISEY - (canary). The Heisey Co., located in Newark, Ohio, began production in 1896. Heisey first produced vaseline in 1899 or 1900. About 1923 or 1924, some items were again produced in vaseline, although production seems to have been experimental. Heisey's vaseline is generally paler than vaseline produced by other companies. Pieces produced in vaseline by Heisey were usually accessory pieces, like vases and compotes. Heisey also sold blanks to other companies, which then added their own decoration. In 1957, the doors were closed to the factory. Its moulds and design patents were transferred to Imperial in 1958.

HOBBS - Hobbs, Brockunier & Co. was located in Wheeling, West Virginia. It was reorganized in 1888 as the Hobbs Glass Co. and became Factory H in the U.S. Glass Co. in 1891.

IMPERIAL - (golden green). The Imperial Glass Co. was organized at Wheeling, West Virginia, in 1901. It began producing glass in

Bellaire, Ohio in 1904. It was noted for carnival and stretch glass. Stretch glass was produced from 1916 to the early 1920s. Imperial was one of the three major producers of American-made stretch glass. In the 1920s , it produced a large line of tableware in colored pattern glass. Golden green was only made for a short time. The company was sold to Lenox, Inc. in 1973 and closed in 1984.

INDIANA TUMBLER & GOBLET CO. - This was originally the Greentown Glass Works in Greentown, Indiana. In 1899, it became part of the National Glass Co. and became the Indiana Tumbler & Goblet Works. It was destroyed by fire in 1903.

JEANNETTE - (canary). The Jeanette Glass Co. (1900-1983) opened originally in the old McKee factory in Jeannette, Pennsylvania. On occasion, Jeannette items turn up in vaseline, even though this wasn't a color in their regular line.

JEFFERSON - The Jefferson Glass Co. was founded in Steubenville, Ohio in 1900. In 1906 it was relocated to Follansbee, West Virginia and the Steubenville plant was sold to the Imperial Glass Co. The factory was closed in the 1930s.

KING - The King Glass Co. was located in Pittsburgh, Pennsylvania. In 1891, it became a part of the U.S. Glass Co., and was known as Factory K.

MCKEE - (canary). McKee and Brothers originated in Pittsburgh, Pennsylvania in 1853. In 1888, it moved to a Pennsylvania community which became known as Jeanette. McKee was noted for its clocks, dispensers, lamps, and crackle glass. After several name changes, it was purchased by the Jeanette Glass Corporation in 1961.

MILLERSBURG - The Millersburg Glass Co. (1909-1914) was located in Millersburg, Ohio. This company was noted for its carnival glass, some of which had a vaseline base. These pieces are quite rare today.

MODEL FLINT - Located in Findlay, Ohio, it was mistakenly referred to as the Novelty Flint Glass Co. in a local paper when it was founded in 1888. In 1893, it was moved to Albany, Indiana. It became a part of the National Glass Co. in 1899 and the name was changed to the Model Flint Glass Works. It was abandoned by National Glass in 1902 and sold in 1908. Canary opalescent glass was produced by Model Flint while operating under National Glass.

MOSSER - Mosser Glass, Inc. was founded about 1964 in Cambridge, Ohio. It is known for its reproduction novelties and tableware.

NATIONAL GLASS - The National Glass Combine was chartered in 1899 and consisted of 19 factories: Beatty-Brady Glass Works; Canton Glass Works; Central Glass Works; Crystal Glass Works; Cumberland Glass Works; Dalzell, Gilmore & Leighton; Fairmont Glass Works; Greensburg Glass Works;Indiana Tumbler & Goblet Works; Keystone Glass Works;Model Flint Glass Works; McKee & Brothers Glass Works; Northwood Glass Works; Ohio Flint Glass Works; Riverside Glass Works; Robinson Glass Works; Rochester Glass Works; Royal Glass Works; and the West Virginia Glass Works.

NEW MARTINSVILLE - (canary). The New Martinsville Glass Manufacturing Co. began in New Martinsville, West Virginia in 1901. In 1924, canary was introduced. In 1944, the company was bought out and renamed the Viking Glass Company. The company was sold in 1986 and operates today as the Dalzell-Viking Glass Co.

NORTHWOOD - H. Northwood and Co. was established in Wheeling, West Virginia, in 1902. Its owner, Harry Northwood, had previously run glass factories in Indiana, Pennsylvania, and elsewhere. They were noted for their pressed and novelty items and were one of the companies which often used a cranberry ruffle with a contrasting color. Northwood also often used hand-painted bands on its carnival and stretch glass. Stretch glass with a baked-on enamel band is usually attributed to Northwood. One of the three main producers of stretch glass in the U.S., Northwood was probably the largest glass company to produce it, making it from 1910-1922, when the company went out of business.

PAIRPOINT - The Pairpoint Mfg. Co. was established in New Bedford, Massachusetts in 1880. It merged with the Mt. Washington Glass Co. in 1894. After several changes in name and ownership, it was relocated in East Wareham, Massachusetts in 1957 and became the Pairpoint Glass Co. the following year, importer of Spanish glass. The factory was reopened in Sagamore, Massachusetts in 1970.

PORTLAND - The Portland Glass Co. was founded in Portland, Maine in 1863. It was destroyed by fire and rebuilt the following year. It was reorganized as the Portland Glass Works in 1870 and closed in 1873.

RICHARDS & HARTLEY - This company was founded in Pittsburgh, Pennsylvania in 1869. In 1881, the company moved to Tarentum, Pennsylvania. They were noted for their pressed wares. In 1891, they became a part of U. S. Glass, and were known as Factory E. The factory was closed in 1893 and later was sold to the Tarentum Glass Co.

RIVERSIDE GLASS WORKS - The Riverside Glass Works was first in operation in 1879, in Wellsburg, West Virginia. It specialized in pressed glassware and was well-known for its line of lamps and the use of gold decoration. Some of its finer patterns in vaseline are Petticoat, Ranson, and Derby. In 1899, Riverside became a part of National Glass Co. In 1904, National Glass Co. leased out the Riverside factory to a stock company. Its name was officially changed to Riverside Glass Co. The factory was closed in 1907, molds and equipment sold to pay creditors or sent to other National Glass Co. plants.

L.E. SMITH - (canary). The L.E. Smith Co. is located in Mt. Pleasant, Pennsylvania. Canary

was introduced in 1926. The company made a line of crackle glass, as well as pattern glass. Some of its patterns are By Cracky and Romanesque. The company continues to operate under new ownership.

STANDARD - (canary). Mainly a cutting and etching firm, the Standard Glass Manufacturing Co. was located near Lancaster, Ohio. It became a subsidiary of Hocking Glass Co. in 1924. In 1925, canary glassware became available.

STEVENS & WILLIAMS - These English glassmakers operated at the Brierly Hill Glassworks, located in Stourbridge, England. The glass I have seen has been noted as Stevens & Williams, rather than by the name of the factory. They were noted for several styles of art glass. The glassworks was in operation from 1847 until quite recently under various owners.

SUMMIT - The Summit Art Glass Co. was founded in Akron, Ohio in 1972. The plant was moved in 1984 to Rootstown, Ohio and is still in operation. It purchased many of its moulds from the St. Clair Glass Works.

U.S. GLASS - (canary). In 1891, 18 glass companies combined to form U.S. Glass. These companies were Adams & Co., Bryce Bros., Challinor, Taylor & Co., George Duncan & Sons, Richards & Hartley, Ripley & Co., Gillinder & Sons, Hobbs Glass Co., Columbia Glass Co., King Glass Co., O'Hara Glass Co., Bellaire Glass Co., Nickel Plate Glass Co., Central Glass Co., Doyle & Co., A.J. Beatty & Sons, and Novelty Glass Co. A large variety of glass was produced at the individual factories. Satin, craquelle, stippled and patterned glassware were all produced in the mid-twenties.

VAL ST. LAMBERT CRISTALLERIES - This factory was established in Belgium in the early 1900s. They produced some very fine Vaseline glassware and are still in operation today. The glassware produced there was similar to Lalique but never achieved the same recognition.

WHEATON - Wheaton Glass was established in Millville, New Jersey in 1888. In the 1970s, Wheatonware sold some vaseline glass through their home party plan. Kemple moulds were used and some collector plates were also made in vaseline.

L.G. WRIGHT - This company was founded in the 1930s in New Martinsville, West Virginia. The company used factories, such as Fenton, to manufacture glass, which it then sold. Bailey, Dalzell-Viking, Davis-Lynch, Fostoria, Gibson, Imperial, Morgantown, Mosser, New Martinsville, Paden City, Plum, Rodefer, Summit, Venetian, Westmoreland, Wilkerson, and Viking were some of the other factories producing glass for L.G. Wright. It is still in operation.

EPILOGUE

The little boy has grown older, but the wonder of the magic glass is as strong today as it was when he made himself a promise to own some of it.

The sunlight setting off flashes of beautiful yellows and greens and the wondrous fluorescent glows in the dark rooms under ultraviolet light still make him reject all the scientific explanations he knows in favor of the simple answer of magic he feels.

There remains only the growing and sad realization that he can't take his toys with him when it's time to go …

— Jay L. Glickman

BIBLIOGRAPHY

Baker, Gary, et. al. *Wheeling Glass, 1829-1939*. Edited by Gerald I Reilly. Wheeling, WV: Oglebay Institute Glass Museum, 1994.

Biser, Benjamin F. *Elements of Glassmaking*. Pittsburgh: Glass and Pottery Publishing Co., 1922.

Bredehoft, Neila. *Collector's Encyclopedia of Heisey Glass 1925-1938*. Paducah, KY: Collector Books, 1986.

Bredehoft, Neila, George A. Fogg, and Francis C. Maloney. *Early Duncan Glassware: George Duncan and Sons, 1876-1892*. Self published, 1987.

Bredehoft, Neila and Tom. *Victorian Novelties and Figurals*: *Geo. Duncan and Sons*. St. Louisville, OH. Cherry Hill Publications, 1989.

D'Imperio, Dan. *The ABC's of Victorian Antiques*. New York: Dodd Mead & Co., 1974.

Edwards, Bill. *The Standard Encyclopedia of Carnival Glass*. Paducah, KY: Collector Books, 1982.

Elira, Mary. *Discovery of the Elements*, 7th edition journal of Chemical Education, 1968.

Finegan, Bill and Eileen. "Vaseline Glass." *Heisey Herald*, Vol. 13, No. 4 (October 1984).

Florence, Gene. *Collector's Encyclopedia of Depression Glass*, 13th edition. Paducah, KY: Collector Books, 1998.

Gorham, C.W. *Riverside Glass Works of Wellsburg, West Virginia 1879-1907*. Springfield, MO: Heartlights, 1995.

Hais, Rudolph. "Bohemian Uranium Glass." *Czech. Glass Review* (October 1988).

Hartung, Marion T. *Opalescent Pattern Glass*. Des Moines: Wallace Homestead, 1971.

Heacock, William. *Encyclopedia of Victorian Colored Pattern Glass, Book II, Opalescent Glass from A to Z*. Marietta, OH: Antique Publications, 1977.

Heacock, William. *Fenton Glass: The Second Twenty-Five Years*. Marietta, OH: Antique Publications, 1980.

Heacock, William. *Fenton Glass: The Third Twenty-Five Years*. Marietta, OH: Antique Publications, 1989.

Heacock, William. *Old Pattern Glass According to Heacock*. Marietta, OH: Antique Publications, 1981.

Heacock, William and Fred Bickenhauser. *Encyclopedia of Victorian Colored Pattern Glass, Book 5, U.S. Glass from A to Z*. Marietta, OH: Antique Publications, 1978.

Heacock, William and William Gamble. *Encyclopedia of Victorian Colored Pattern Glass, Book 9, Cranberry Opalescent from A to Z*. Marietta, OH: Antique Publications, 1987.

Heacock, William, James Measell, and Berry Wiggins. *Dugan/Diamond: The Story of Indiana, Pennsylvania, Glass*. Marietta, OH: Antique Publications, 1993.

Heacock, William, James Measell, and Berry Wiggins. *Harry Northwood: The Early Years, 1881-1900*. Marietta, OH: Antique Publications, 1990.

Heacock, William, James Measell, and Berry Wiggins. *Harry Northwood: The Wheeling Years, 1901-1925*. Marietta, OH: Antique Publications, 1991.

Hecht, Eugene and Alfred Zajac. *Optics*. Reading, MA., 1987.

Hughes, G. Bernard. *English Glass for the Collector, 1660-1860*. New York: MacMillan Co., 1958.

Husfloen, Kyle. *Collector's Guide to American Pressed Glass, 1825-1915*. Radnor, PA: Wallace-Homestead, 1992.

Innes, Lowell. *Pittsburgh Glass 1797-1891*. Boston: Houghton Mifflin Co. 1976.

Jenks, Bill and Jerry Luna. *Early American Pattern Glass, 1850-1910*. Radnor, PA: Wallace-Homestead, 1990.

Kovar, Lorraine. *Westmoreland Glass, 1950-1984*. Marietta, OH: Antique Publications, 1991.

Lattimore, Colin. *English 19th-Century Press-Moulded Glass*. London: Barrie & Jenkins, 1979.

Lee, Ruth Webb. *Antique Fakes and Reproductions*. Framingham Center, MA, 1952.

McKearin, G. and H. *American Glass*. New York: Crown, 1972.

Measell, James, editor. *Fenton Glass: The 1980s Decade*. Marietta, OH: Antique Publications, 1995.

Measell, James, editor. *Imperial Glass Encyclopedia, Vol. I, A-Cane*. Marietta, OH: Antique Publications, 1995.

Measell, James, editor. *Imperial Glass Encyclopedia, Vol. II, Cape Cod-L*. Marietta, OH: Antique Publications, 1997.

Measell, James and W.C. "Red" Roetteis. *The L.G.Wright Glass Company*. Marietta, OH: Antique Publications, 1997.

Michols, Edward L. and Ernest Merritt. "Studies in Luminescence." *Phys. Review*, Vol. 19 (1904).

National Cambridge Collectors, Inc. *Colors in Cambridge Glass*. Paducah, KY: Collector Books, 1984.

National Cambridge Collectors, Inc. *The Cambridge Glass Co. 1930-1934, Cambridge, Ohio.* Paducah, KY: Collector Books, 1975; Reprinted 1997.

Newbound, Betty. *The Glass Collector's Almanac.* Commerce, MI: self published, 1987.

Newman, Harold. *An Illustrated Dictionary of Glass.* London: Thames and Hudson, 1977.

Pickvet, Mark. *Official Price Guide to Glassware.* New York: House of Collectibles, 1995.

Piña, Leslie, and Jerry Gallagher. *Tiffin Glass 1914-1940.* Atglen, PA: Schiffer Publishing Ltd., 1996.

Powell, Harry J. *The Principles of Glass Making.* London: George Bell & Sons, 1883.

Stout, Sandra. *Complete Book of McKee Glass.* W. Kansas City: The Trojan Press, 1972.

Stout, Sandra. *Heisey on Parade.* Lombard, IL: Wallace-Homestead Book Company, 1985.

Teal, Ron, Sr. *Albany Glass: Model Flint Glass Company of Albany, Indiana.* Marietta, OH: Antique Publications, 1997.

Thuro, Catherine. *Oil Lamps: The Kerosene Era in North America.* Des Moines: Wallace-Homestead, 1976.

Umbraco, Kitty & Russell. *Iridescent Stretch Glass.* Berkeley, CA: Cembura and Avery, 1972.

Weatherman, Hazel Marie. *Colored Glassware of the Depression Era 2.* Ozark, MO: Weatherman Glassbooks, 1974.

Welker, John & Elizabeth. *Pressed Glass in America: Encyclopedia of the First Hundred Years, 1825-1925.* Ivyland, PA: Antique Acres Press, 1985.

Welker, Mary, Lyle, and Lynn. *Cambridge Glass in Color, Book II.* New Concord, OH: privately printed, 1973.

Whitmyer, Margaret and Kenn. *Fenton Art Glass.* Paducah, KY: Collector Books, 1996.

Wills, Geoffrey. *Victorian Glass.* London: George Bell & Sons, n.d.

Yalom, Libby. *Shoes of Glass.* Marietta, OH: Antique Publications, 1988.

Young, Matt. *Optics and Lasers*, 3rd edition. Berlin: Springer-Verlag, 1984.

ABOUT THE AUTHORS

Jay L. Glickman, a collector of Vaseline glass for more than 30 years, has spent many hours researching both the history and the physical-chemical characteristics of his favorite glass.

The holder of several patents on tools for repairing glass, Jay works with glass in his job as an optical lab technician. He also markets and distributes ultraviolet lights for verification of antiques. He lives in Pennsylvania.

His article, "Vaseline Glass—A Collector's Dream!" was featured in the August/September 1989 issue of *Glass Collector's Digest*.

Terry L. Fedosky developed an interest in glassware in the early Seventies, while working for Wheatonware, a subsidiary of Wheaton Glass. She has actively collected Vaseline glass since 1991, although her first pieces were bookends made for Wheatonware from Kemple moulds.

Terry has written several articles for antique publications and served as an advisor on Vaseline glass for an annual price guide. She has appeared with some of her glass on a local news segment and has had some of her favorite pieces on display at a local library.

1998 VALUE GUIDE
YELLOW-GREEN VASELINE:
A GUIDE TO THE MAGIC GLASS (REVISED)

The values given in this guide reflect observations made at numerous antique shows and auctions. Prices may, of course, vary from region to region within the country, but genuine Vaseline glass is scarce everywhere. Prices given are for items in mint condition.

It is a sound investment to obtain and use a portable ultra-violet light to verify genuine Vaseline glass. If you're buying by mail, let the seller know that you will test your purchase immediately with ultra-violet when it arrives. Insist on a return privilege.

All numbered pieces in the color section are priced below. Every effort has been made to suggest fair and reasonable prices, although you will find that actual selling prices vary widely from place to place. These figures are intended only as a guide. Neither the authors nor the publishers can be responsible for losses incurred by those using this value guide as the basis for any sale or other transaction.

1-	$ 430	22-	105	42-	90	63-	395	83-	110
2-	320	23-	140	43-	35 ea	64-	55	84-	90
3-	150	24-	180	44-	185	65-	50	85-	160
4-	265	25-	70	45-	50	66-	90	86-	160
5-	235	26-	175	46-	60	67-	55	87-	195
6-	220, pr	27-	135	47-	65	68-	230	88-	415
7-	120	28-	95	48-	75	69-	125	89-	135
8-	285	29-	55	49-	45	70-	45	90-	120
9-	425	30-	120	50-	400	71-	85	91-	125
10-	130	31-	485	51-	65	72-	95	92-	280
11-	195	32-	60	52-	250	73-	195	93-	495
12-	1850, pr	33-	145	53-	95	74-	220	94-	145
13-	750	34-	40	54-	85	75-	155	95-	115
14-	190	35-	145	55-	150	76-	425	96-	125
15-	110	36-	280	56-	105	77-	140	97-	70
16/17-	225	37-	125	57/58-	285	78-	130	98-	35
18-	95	38-	195	59-	280	79-	225, pr	99-	45
19-	85	39-	180	60-	115	80-	135	100-	90
20-	95	40-	45	61-	275	81-	150	101-	110
21-	80	41-	140	62-	145	82-	155	102-	135

103-	115	137-	155	171-	75	206-	60	240-	210
104-	175	138-	240	172-	195	207-	115	241-	110
105-	165	139-	650	173-	300	208-	95	242-	85
106-	190	140-	195	174-	295	209-	50	243-	125, pr
107-	295	141-	115, pr	175-	260, pr	210-	100	244-	85
108-	525	142-	110	176-	365	211-	75	245-	65
109-	240	143-	320, pr	177-	290, pr	212-	60	246-	75
110-	320	144-	80	178-	135	213-	90	247-	65
111-	365	145-	70	179-	335	214-	115	248-	55
112-	285	146-	110, pr	180-	195	215-	80	249-	45
113-	160	147-	85	181-	165	216-	85	250-	75, pr
114-	495	148-	95	182-	185	217-	110	251-	55
115-	465	149-	55	183-	250	218-	45	252-	80
116-	425	150-	145	184-	95	219-	35	253-	85
117-	415	151-	125	185-	110	220-	40	254-	80
118-	555	152-	120	186-	250	221-	95	255-	80
119-	555	153-	295	187-	95	222-	25	256-	55
120-	400	154-	70	188-	85	223-	45	257-	120, pr
121-	140	155-	115, pr	189-	75	224-	35	258-	95
122-	525, pr	156-	55	190-	220, pr	225-	90, pr	259-	75
123-	325	157-	170	191-	130	226-	110	260-	95
124-	415	158-	95	192-	125	227-	195	261-	60
125-	95	159-	165	193-	110	228-	165, pr	262-	60
126-	180	160-	150	194-	135	229-	75	263-	55
127-	200	161-	85	195-	435	230-	125	264-	55
128-	195	162-	55	196-	510	231-	70	265-	45
129-	245	163-	70	197/98	625	232-	95	266-	80
130-	265	164-	85	199-	215	233-	95	267-	45
131-	125, pr	165-	35	200-	445	234-	70	268-	20
132-	70, pr	166-	180	201-	90	235-	125	269-	35
133-	120	167-	70	202-	85	236-	65	270-	125
134-	65	168-	80	203-	325	237-	245	271-	45
135-	160	169-	120	204-	130	238-	55	272-	45
136-	240	170-	75	205-	85	239-	120	273-	45

274-	120	309-	75	343-	25	377-	85	412-	30
275-	200	310-	85	344-	25	378-	85	413-	45
276-	450	311-	195	345-	60	379-	25	414-	45
277-	125, pr	312-	95	346-	58	380-	15	415-	60
278-	110, pr	313-	25	347-	35	381-	15	416-	45
279-	55	314-	35	348-	55	382-	30	417-	30
280-	95 A&B	315-	25	349-	55	383-	30	418-	30
281-	55	316-	55	350-	55	384-	30	419-	45
282/83 -120		317-	25	351-	50	385-	40	420-	50
284-	60	318-	200	352-	50	386-	55	421-	20
285-	85	319-	225	353-	35	387-	65	422-	45
286-	55	320-	145	354-	30	388-	35	423-	40
287-	190	321-	75	355-	30	389-	35	424-	20
288-	1100	322-	145	356-	75	390-	55	425-	45
289-	135	323-	65	357-	18	391-	30	426-	35
290-	115	324-	625	358-	25	392-	30	427-	85
291-	85	325-	675	359-	20	393-	45	428-	45
292-	95	326-	45	360-	18	394-	35	429-	25
293-	135	327-	155	361-	45	395-	30	430-	30
294-	95	328-	30	362-	40	396-	55	431-	20
295-	115	329-	35	363-	35	397/398- 85		432-	395/520, pr
296-	120, pr	330-	45	364-	35	399-	55	433-	175, ea
297-	310	331-	45	365-	45	400-	45	434-	550
298-	95	332-	45	366-	45	401-	45	435-	525
299-	95	333-	95	367-	50	402-	60	436-	NA
300-	145	334-	55	368-	85	403-	75	437-	NA
301-	75	335-	25	369-	80	404-	45	438-	235
302-	30	336-	35	370-	125	405-	35	439-	195
303-	25	337-	45	371-	75	406-	75	440-	380
304-	15	338-	35	372-	60	407-	20	441-	175
305-	15	339-	35	373-	25	408-	25	442-	135
306-	20	340-	40	374-	25	409-	55	443-	525
307-	85	341-	75, pr	375-	60	410-	75	444-	55
308-	55	342-	95, pr	376-	145	411-	50	445-	70

446-	45	477-	185	510-	40	543-	40	576-	20
447-	60	478-	35	511-	45	544-	95	577-	26
448-	90, pr	479-	100	512-	40	545-	55	578-	35
449-	135	480-	50	513-	40	546-	45, ea	579-	25
450-	145	481-	95	514-	50	547-	75	580-	25
451-	45, pr	482-	120	515-	45	548-	40	581-	28
452-	165	483-	50	516-	75	549-	35	582-	30
453-	95	484-	60	517-	145	550-	15	583-	35
454-	60	485-	120	518-	110	551-	65	584-	28
455-	60	486-	75	519-	135	552-	75, pr.	585-	35
456-	45	487-	75	520-	25	553-	75	586-	20
457-	95	488-	85	521-	85	554-	45	587-	30
		489-	70	522-	60	555-	45, pr.	588-	26

SUPPLEMENT PRICE GUIDE

		490-	85	523-	85	556-	28	589-	30
458-	400	491-	90	524-	55	557-	60	590-	26
459-	450	492-	110	525-	19	558-	12, ea	591-	18
460-	60	493-	68	526-	20	559-	30, ea	592-	55
461-	95	494-	65	527-	45	560-	30	593-	25
462-	75	495-	85	528-	55	561-	25		
463-	85	496-	45	529-	45	562-	45		
464-	55	497-	35	530-	60	563-	25		
465-	85	498-	30	531-	125	564-	35		
466-	75	499-	65	532-	55	565-	25		
467-	55	500-	75	533-	55	566-	55		
468-	55	501-	50	534-	95	567-	35		
469-	50	502-	60	535-	85	568-	45		
470-	95	503-	50	536-	55	569-	20		
471-	100	504-	45	537-	50	570-	45		
472-	85	505-	75	538-	110	571-	30		
473-	45	506-	85	539-	45	572-	25		
474-	60	507-	80	540-	85	573-	45		
475-	140	508-	35	541-	45	574-	30		
476-	65	509-	65	542-	35	575-	25		